D0205683

Twayne's Theatrical Arts Series

Warren French
EDITOR

Sydney Pollack

Sydney Pollack

Sydney Pollack

WILLIAM R. TAYLOR

BOSTON

Twayne Publishers

1981

Sydney Pollack

Published in 1981 by Twayne Publishers,
A Division of G. K. Hall & Co.

Printed on permanent/durable acid-free paper and bound
in the United States of America

First Printing, June 1981
Frontispiece photo courtesy of Sydney Pollack

Library of Congress Cataloging in Publication Data

Taylor, William Robert, 1942–
Sydney Pollack.

(Twayne's theatrical arts series)
Bibliography: p.161
Filmography: p.162–67
Includes index.
1. Pollack, Sydney, 1934–
PN1998.A3P5926 791.43′0233′0924 80-39800
ISBN 0-8057-9279-1

Contents

About the Author

WILLIAM ROBERT TAYLOR, born in Hartford, Connecticut, received a Bachelor of Science degree in education and English from the University of Hartford in 1964, a Master of Arts degree in English from the University of Vermont in 1968, and a Certificate of Advanced Study in literature and film from Wesleyan University in 1978. He has taught English at Coventry and Waterford high schools in Connecticut. At Waterford, Mr. Taylor initiated a filmmaking course which was to lead him into taking graduate courses in film at Wesleyan.

At Wesleyan, he studied film with Jeanine Basinger, author of *Anthony Mann* for the Twayne Series. After deciding to pursue Sydney Pollack's work in film for a thesis project, Mr. Taylor met with him, and was later invited to spend a week in Las Vegas in order to observe some of the filming of *The Electric Horseman*.

Mr. Taylor was a Visiting Lecturer in Film Studies for the Graduate Summer School at Wesleyan, and he taught a course which centered on Pollack's work. He also lectured in a public film series at Wesleyan, and Mr. Pollack came to the university to speak at one of the lectures. Mr. Taylor's plans for the future include working on a book about the individuals who are a part of the film-production crew.

Editor's Foreword

ONE OF THE SPECIAL goals of this series has been to provide books about significant contemporary creators of American film, especially with the collaboration of the subjects. Curiously, a symposium about Sydney Pollack was published in France ten years ago, after the enthusiastic reception in Europe of *They Shoot Horses, Don't They?*; but this study by William R. Taylor is the first detailed critique of Pollack's substantial and provocative body of work to appear in the United States.

Pollack's films are from one viewpoint difficult to deal with because of a lack of continuity and predictability in his subject matter. He cannot be stereotyped as a practitioner of any particular genre; indeed he has restlessly experimented so far in nearly every familiar genre—mystery-suspense *(The Slender Thread, Three Days of the Condor)*, traditional Western *(The Scalphunters, Jeremiah Johnson)*, film noir *(They Shoot Horses)*, southern gothic *(This Property Is Condemned)*, fantasy *(Castle Keep)*, sports romance *(Bobby Deerfield)*. Although *The Way We Were* and *The Yakuza* cannot be labeled "musical" and "Kung Fu" films in the usual senses, the former is often remembered for its haunting theme song, while the latter has the Oriental trappings of the exotic genre. Pollack tried his hand, in short, at nearly everything that was being done in the 1960s and 1970s except catastrophe films and space epics (such stereotyped substitution of special effects for character study would be especially distasteful to the kind of filmmaker we shall find Pollack is).

In view of this seemingly formless diversity, William Taylor has perceptively chosen not to prepare a chronological series of critiques of Pollack's films, but rather to organize his discussion around the elements of similarity beneath this diversity, pointing out the continuing preoccupations that united Pollack's films as the products of a controlling central intelligence.

This study is, however, finally even more thorough than the preceding summary suggests; for Taylor actually achieves the rounded view possible by counterpointing two approaches. The first is a chronological study of the development of Pollack's increasingly subtle visual art from his beginnings in television through *Bobby Deerfield*, while the second is a series of linked essays on circular structures in the film, comments on the American tradition, and the heroes, heroines, and villains that have provided the stabilizing continuity between films as Pollack has refined his visual style and moved among a variety of geographical and historical settings. Then, in a final chapter on *The Electric Horseman*, Taylor tests his observations by applying them to one of Pollack's most popular and ingratiating films, in which he works again with two favorite stars, Robert Redford and Jane Fonda, to create a modern variation on the legendary Western.

Throughout the book still another dimension is added to the analysis by extended quotations from Pollack's conversations with the author, in which the director talks about the way he works and what he hopes to accomplish in his film. What emerges from this complex structure is evidence that it is indeed possible, though difficult, to be an *auteur* in Hollywood today, to bring to the screen stories that embody a consistent, somewhat sentimental, yet uncompromising vision of the American experience.

What also emerges, even more importantly, is a three-dimensional picture of a new kind of director. The imperial figures of the studio era like Cecil B. De Mille and Alfred Hitchcock no longer prevail. We see Pollack as rather a diplomatic and considerate leader of a team the director depends upon from film to film to give consistent final form to projects that are constantly subject to revision as they are in progress. (Just as Pollack's films are more admired in Europe than in the United States, his methods more nearly resemble those of famous European directors than those of most of his American colleagues.)

One can not help feeling finally that one of the reasons for the unity underlying Pollack's outwardly diverse work is that he has much in common with many of his heroes, epitomized by Sonny Steele in *The Electric Horseman*, who are often fed up with a frustrating world around them but still determined to get a job done right. Much less flamboyantly than Francis Ford Coppola, Pollack has persisted in making "personal films"; and so long as determined individuals can find the means to make such films, film study will remain an increasingly significant part of humanistic concerns in an increasingly visually oriented age.

W. F.

Preface

FOR YEARS I went through life blissfully unaware that any such thing as the *auteur* theory existed—let alone that it was something applied to movies. As an English teacher, I was perfectly certain that movies were an extension of literature; add in aspects of the dramatic arts, and you have a film! Well, perhaps there might be an artistic side to film, but that was reserved for those strange foreign films. What does *auteur* have to do with American films, anyhow?

Then came one graduate course called "Six American Film Directors" taught by one Jeanine Basinger at Wesleyan University. So I get to watch a lot of movies and write a couple of papers. Not that simple! A rapid six weeks convinced me that good films are primarily the result of good film directors, but it also taught me that writing about film was more demanding than I ever thought possible. I was learning to verbalize that which I had always felt, although I never had the means to express it. Thank you, Jeanine.

Another course, and I was thoroughly hooked on films. I could spot a Capra, a Sturges, or a Hawks. I was beginning to "see," while before I had only "looked." With new eyes set firmly in place, I went to see *Three Days of the Condor* because Tina Chen was in it—fellow graduate of the University of Hartford. Amazing film—the director, Sydney Pollack.

With heightened interest in Pollack's work, I sought titles of his previous films. *Jeremiah Johnson* and *They Shoot Horses, Don't They?* stood out in the list. I could still vividly remember whole scenes from both movies. Research proved that little of any substance had been written about Pollack, so a thesis topic was born.

Through an interview granted in New York City while Pollack was looping *Bobby Deerfield*, I came to know a most personable and articulate film director who was more than willing to help me in my understanding of his work.

I had been concerned about the *auteur* theory as it applied to Pollack's work since I could not find any identifiable visual style which ran throughout all of the films. I saw many other areas of "authorship," though, which began to convince me that Pollack had a substantial influence in each of his films. There was an absolute crossover in structure, treatment of the major characters, and in the careful attention to the composition in the frame, but I wasn't comfortable about Pollack as the author of his films until I went to Las Vegas to watch some of the filming of *The Electric Horseman*.

Pollack's sense of authorship has everything to do with the kind of person he is, and in Las Vegas I came to a clear understanding of the working relationship that he had with all of the individuals in the production unit.

Before traveling to Las Vegas, I was well aware of his working on the scripts of his films. He and I had talked about his writing scenes for *Jeremiah Johnson*, and he had told me about his involvement with the script of *Julia*, but I had never seen him in action. Each night while others were taking a break from the day's work, Pollack was in his room working on the script with the writers and, at times, with Redford. While most of the substantive changes occurred in the evening, minor changes were being made each day. Looking for a funnier line for Sonny Steele when he is promoting Ranch Breakfast, Redford, during one of the takes, came up with "peas" as an additional food whose nutritional value was found in the cereal. The script was evolving; it was a living unit which was finding its evolution through the influence of several while under the direction of one.

In Associated Press releases which appeared shortly before the premiere of *Horseman*, headlines proclaimed Pollack's breaking a fundamental law of filmmaking by starting to shoot without first completing the script. When Pollack reverses this tendency, he will lose much of his value as a creative force. What he does, and does well, in his creative process is to use the insight of the professionals who surround him. This is not to say that he has not very carefully considered every aspect of the film, but rather that by asking those around him to discuss their responses, he gains the best part of their knowledge while showing his respect for their knowledge as well.

Pollack makes the final decisions; the choices are ultimately his, but when he treats all with respect for their professional judgment, they characteristically try their best to please him. In talking with Stephen Grimes, the production designer for six of Pollack's films starting with *This Property Is Condemned* in 1966, I learned that the design may begin with Pollack in the abstract, but then it is turned over to Grimes so that he can give it more tangible form. It may be finding the best alley for *Condor*, the best canyon for *Horseman*, or the most appropriate look for Wheat's house in *Yakuza*. After working in partnership with Pollack on six films, Grimes knows what Pollack is looking for; he is able to create the "look" while satisfying both his and Pollack's judgments because they understand each other on a professional level.

All the members of the production unit communicate with Pollack. They always have access to him. Although they may be ultimately working for him, they are first working with him on the film.

While standing in a lunch line one day, I was told that Pollack was faced with serious financial problems near the end of the filming of *Jeremiah Johnson*, but rather than cutting costs, which would affect the crew's morale, Pollack put some of his personal assets on the line. The crew continued to eat steak rather than hamburger. It doesn't sound like much, but given such a relationship between the director and the production unit, it is no small surprise that all would do everything in their power to give Pollack what he had requested.

After my week in Las Vegas, I could understand Sydney Pollack as the author of his films even though so many people were involved in the total film process.

In an effort to present Pollack as the author of his films, I have taken the most visible areas of his influence—visual art, American themes, structures, heroes, heroines, and villains—as subjects for the chapters of this book. This organization of the material, I believe, offers a better insight into Pollack's work than a film-by-film analysis would although the second chapter on visual style is organized chronologically to orient the study. While audiences necessarily look at single units of a director's work, I have attempted to pull all of the films together even if it first means taking them apart. Drawing close comparisons between films which at first seem totally opposite—*Bobby Deerfield* and *Jeremiah Johnson*, for instance—can only be accomplished by looking at their component parts.

For the most part, the subjects of each of the chapters emanated from my interviews with Pollack. As I began to understand his philosophic outlooks on life, I began to see their applications in his films.

Preface

The quotations appearing at the beginning of each of the chapters are taken primarily from my interviews with Pollack; they served as the catalysts for my attempts to understand his influence in each of his films.

If it were not for Pollack's interest in my project, and if it were not for his accessibility to me, I could not have approached this task with such confidence. In thanking him, I also thank Bernardine Kent, his assistant and the choreographer for *The Electric Horseman*. In the midst of chaos, whether on location or at the office, Bernie always managed (cheerfully, even) to provide me with the information that I needed.

As this production comes to a close, I as the author of another sort must give credit to my own production crew. My wife, Eunice, who willingly worked two jobs so that I could study film at Wesleyan, and who was a constant source of encouragement and assistance; Jeanine Basinger, who started me off and then kept me going in film; Gail DiMaggio, my perceptive and honest critic of rough drafts; Cheryl and John Egan, good East Coast friends who cared; Sally and Ralph Melton, good West Coast friends and "good ole" people who not only put up with me but also put me up; and my daughter, Kristin, who did her four-year-old best to assure me that everything would be all right.

WILLIAM R. TAYLOR

Acknowledgments

A book on Sydney Pollack without the corresponding images of his art would be as absurd as my not acknowledging those who made the inclusion of stills possible: Mary Corliss of the Museum of Modern Art/Film Stills Archives, 11 W. 53rd St., New York; Paula Klaw Kramer of Movie Star News, 212 E. 14th St., New York; and John Bryson of Malibu, California, who was on location in Japan for the filming of *The Yakuza*, as well as—most generously—the director himself. Additionally, I thank Columbia Pictures for granting me permission to use their stills as well.

Chronology

1934 Sidney Irwin Pollack born on July 1 in Lafayette, Indiana, the oldest of three children of David and Rebecca Pollack.

1947- Introduced to drama by James Lewis Casaday at South Bend
1952 Central High School.

1952 Moves to New York City and studies under Sanford Meisner at the Neighborhood Playhouse.

1953 Receives a fellowship to continue at the Playhouse; becomes Meisner's assistant; begins teaching private classes in acting; has a role in the Broadway production of *A Stone for Danny Fisher;* appears in many television dramas.

1957 Drafted into the army; serves at Fort Carson, Colorado.

1958 Marries former acting student Claire Griswold; they eventually have three children: Steven Sanford, Rebecca Jeff, and Rachel Mary.

1959 Returns to the Neighborhood Playhouse.

1960- Goes to Hollywood as a dialogue coach for John Frankenhei-
1961 mer's *The Young Savages;* becomes involved with direction through Burt Lancaster's influence; directs most major television shows; appears in *War Hunt* with Robert Redford.

1965 *The Slender Thread.*

1966 *This Property Is Condemned.*

1967 *The Scalphunters.*

1968 *Castle Keep.*

1970 *They Shoot Horses, Don't They?*, also coproducer; the picture receives nine Academy Award nominations including Best Direction; wins Best Picture and Best Director awards at the Yugoslavian Film Festival; wins a Special Prize at the Cannes Film Festival; wins the Belgium Film Festival Award; receives the Jury Prize at the Moscow Film Festival; wins the Director's Guild Award for Outstanding Achievement in Film Direction.

1972 *Jeremiah Johnson*, also coproducer; world premiere at the Cannes Film Festival.
1973 *The Way We Were:* receives six Academy Award nominations, winning two in music.
1974 *The Yakuza*, also producer.
1975 *Three Days of the Condor*, also producer.
1977 *Bobby Deerfield*, also producer.
1979 *The Electric Horseman.*
1980 Produces *Honeysuckle Rose;* begins filming *Absence of Malice.*

1

The Man behind the Image

"When I first began, I didn't have any control in the sense that I do now, but if your argument is better than somebody elses's, you can exercise an enormous amount of control. In a curious kind of way, you may be able to get exactly what you want not with muscle, but with politics or diplomacy"

—Sydney Pollack.

* *

The story of Sydney Pollack's rise to prominence as a Hollywood film director is complete with the details of fortunate timing and liaisons with important people in the industry; yet, Pollack's ability to maintain his position lends credence to his strength as a director and to his ability to maintain a balance between artistic inclination and the demands of multi-million-dollar film projects. Roughly, Pollack's movement from South Bend, Indiana, to Burbank, California, is divided into four periods: his early life in South Bend, his New York experience as a student and teacher of acting, his Hollywood involvement before the filming of *They Shoot Horses, Don't They?*, and his career in film following the completion of that movie.

South Bend seems a most unlikely environment for fostering the creative inclinations of one sensitive to art; as Pollack has commented, "my essential memories of South Bend were not happy memories. It was not a town where I felt at home, or comfortable. It was not a town that encouraged creativity—it was a town without culture." Pollack was born July 1, 1934, in Lafayette, Indiana, where his parents, David and Rebecca, attended Purdue University. A former professional boxer, David Pollack was to own a pharmacy in an immigrant section of South Bend. Rebecca Pollack's activities in the arts, as a singer of Russian folksongs and a piano player, were those which her three chil-

Photo: Sydney Pollack choreographs a fight scene during the filming of The Yakuza. *(courtesy of Sydney Pollack)*

dren were to follow. The second child, Bernie, has established himself as a costume designer, and the third, Sharon, is a choreographer.

Sydney Pollack's years in South Bend were replete with the problems facing any youth, but they were perhaps intensified by the overt racism which existed in a town having a small Jewish population, and by the extended illness of his mother, who died when he was seventeen.

Pollack's junior and senior high-school years reflected the divergent interests of his parents. "I felt confused most of the time. I tried hard to play football, and had some success mostly because I was a fast runner, but I was handicapped by my vision and was actually a better runner than a football player." His mother's interests, however, were manifested in all of her children by their involvement in drama while they attended high school.

Several individuals played important roles in bringing Pollack to a career in film. The first, James Lewis Casaday, taught the drama class at South Bend Central High School. Through Casaday's guidance, and through the trips to Chicago which he initiated, Casaday introduced Pollack to performances of ballet and to other cultural activities which a boy from South Bend would be unlikely to experience. As a result of Casaday's recognition of Pollack's talent and Pollack's resultant expanded interest in the theater, Pollack decided to seek a theatrical career. Calling his action "one of my best memories of South Bend," Pollack boarded the train to New York City following his graduation from high school.

He enrolled in the Neighborhood Playhouse under the direction of Sanford Meisner, who was to become Pollack's second important mentor in the dramatic arts. As Pollack has noted, "the Neighborhood Playhouse was a profound experience. People were concerned with things that I felt, but could never articulate." Meisner's influence on Pollack was then, and remains today, profound. "I learned more about everything from him—life, art, acting, directing, writing. I still fall back on everything I learned there, whether I'm in a script conference, working with an actor, editing a film, or anywhere else."

Facing the daily financial demands of living in New York was difficult, but with some money saved through childhood jobs, the weekly benevolence of an aunt, a summer spent in a South Bend lumber yard, and small roles in television shows, Pollack had enough money to remain at the Playhouse. When he returned to New York for his second year with Meisner, he was given a fellowship, and he soon had a role in his first Broadway show, *A Stone for Danny Fisher,* at age nineteen. He increased his earnings when he started to teach private classes in acting in a rented room at the Playhouse, and he was becoming financially self-sustaining.

Pollack's agents at the time, the Music Corporation of America, employed Eleanor Killgallan and Monique James, now vice-presidents of Universal Studios in the New Talent Department. Pollack recalls that they "were like mothers to me. They worried about everything—they would call to see if I had enough to eat—they would scrounge me a job somewhere if I needed money." In addition to Pollack, another of their "finds" was Robert Redford.

By 1955–56, Pollack was gaining a reputation both as an actor and as a teacher of actors. He appeared in *The Dark is Light Enough* with Katherine Cornell and Tyrone Power, and toured the East in *Stalag 17*. He also appeared in most of the major live television shows of the time: "Playhouse 90," "Kraft Television Theatre," "Goodyear Playhouse," "Alcoa Presents," and others. Then he was drafted.

If anything positive were to come out of this crucial interruption in his acting career, it was Pollack's return on leave to New York in 1958 to marry one of his former acting students, Claire Griswold. They moved to Fort Carson, Colorado, for the duration of Pollack's service obligation, and then later returned to New York to try to reestablish his acting career.

The return to acting was difficult. New actors had moved up in the ranks during Pollack's absence; it was necessary to begin again to establish the reputation which he had before being drafted. Pollack returned to the Neighborhood Playhouse to teach—not because of his interest in teaching, but because of his desire to continue the close working relationship with Sanford Meisner. He also resumed the pursuit of his acting career. In 1958, Pollack read for a part in *For Whom the Bell Tolls*, a two-part "Playhouse 90" production of Hemingway's novel being directed by John Frankenheimer.

Frankenheimer was to become the next major influence in Pollack's career. He was given a role in the production and received a much-needed and substantial salary for his involvement in the six weeks of production. Frankenheimer had studied with Meisner while Pollack was at Fort Carson, and when during the production he learned that Pollack was Meisner's assistant, another opportunity arose.

About to direct Ingrid Bergman in her first television appearance in the United States in Henry James's *The Turn of the Screw*, Frankenheimer asked Pollack to coach two youngsters who were to be in the play. The difficulty with the task, as Pollack offers, was that "I could not interfere conceptually with his direction of the project. I managed to help the kids but not get in Frankenheimer's way. Later, when he did his first picture with Burt Lancaster in 1960, *The Young Savages*, he invited me to come to California to be the dialogue director and coach three kids who had minimal acting experience, but important roles in the film.

"Burt Lancaster and I became friendly on the set, and he pushed me over into direction. He called Universal Studios to see if they had a training program. They had none, but they agreed to let me observe for six months. At the end of that time they would decide whether or not to take a chance on letting me direct a show. I absorbed as much as I could, and collected $100 a week during this period."

As timing would have it, the television program "Shotgun Slade" was canceled with four shows yet to produce when Pollack finished his observership. Given the opportunity to direct one of the remaining segments, he comments, "I screwed it up royally, but I did learn a lot from the editor, Dick Belding, now head of editorial at Universal. He taught me a lot about the mechanics of film."

Pollack remained in California, and in the fall of 1960 he began to direct most of the major television shows of that time. He directed several segments of "Ben Casey," "The Defenders," "Naked City," and "Dr. Kildare." As he continued to work in direction, he became more comfortable as a director.

Through his work with "Ben Casey" and "Chrysler Theatre," Pollack was beginning to establish himself as a director of note. A two-part "Ben Casey" entitled "A Cardinal Act of Mercy" received five Emmy nominations and won the Emmy for Kim Stanley and Glenda Farrell. "Something About Lee Wiley" for the "Chrysler Theatre" won three nominations including Best Director. "The Game," also for the "Chrysler Theatre," won five nominations, and it won Emmys for Cliff Robertson as Best Actor and Pollack as Best Director.

Shelley Winters won the Emmy in 1964 for Best Actress in Pollack's episode of the "Chrysler Theatre" production of "Two Is the Number." The production also was the first and only American television show at that time to win First Prize at the International Festival of Television Programs at Monte Carlo.

In the midst of his work in television direction, Pollack also gained a role in the movie *War Hunt* in 1960. His agents continued to be Monique James and Eleanor Killgallan, along with Bill Kelly. He met

Robert Redford through his work in this film, and the two of them began a friendship which has endured through the years. To date they have worked on five films together. *War Hunt* was to be Pollack's only screen appearance other than his Hitchcock-like quick appearances in some of his own films.

In 1963 Pollack supervised the English dubbing of Luchino Visconti's *The Leopard* at the request of Burt Lancaster, who had starred in the film.

In looking back at his work in television, Pollack reflects: "It was a great and thorough training ground. Now I spend a year and a half on a picture. I'm different when I finish it than when I started it. It takes so damn long; I don't know whether it's going to work or not until a year after I start to work on it. In television I could get an assignment on Monday; the following Monday I was on the floor directing, and two weeks later it was on the air. If it was no good, I could do another one the next week still fresh from last week's lessons. I wasn't reluctant to experiment—it wasn't so serious if one failed. You weren't as worried about falling on your ass because the consequences weren't as severe. You weren't spending six or seven million dollars; you were filling up 'x' number of hours of programmed entertainment, so if you wanted to experiment, you could do it. In the course of five years, I did a hundred shows—a hundred hours of film. I tried everything. I got all the razzle-dazzle out of my system so that I didn't have to do it once I began directing. I had bored myself with wide angle lenses and shooting up noses, and hand-held cameras, and all the things one gets enamored with in the beginning."

As Pollack became a television director of some stature, he began to receive film scripts. In 1965 he decided to try *The Slender Thread* "because it seemed like a big television show—which was one of its faults. It didn't seem too ambitious to try the first time out."

The Slender Thread has visual strengths in offering visual complements to the themes like all of Pollack's films, but it also betrays his recent association with television. As an example, the camera movement of the film when projected onto a large screen illustrates Pollack's having directed for small television screens in the recent past.

Having a very limited viewing area, a television screen necessarily fills only a small part of the viewer's field of vision. If there are to be rapid camera movements, they are offset by the stability which surrounds the television set itself. Such "anchoring" does not hold true for movies. The field of vision for each individual in a film audience is almost totally the image which appears on the large screen. The closer the individual sits to the screen, the more the image becomes his total reality.

The darkness of the movie theater, in contrast to the usual lighting in a television room, also intensifies the projected image as reality. In a movie theater, then, members of the audience have significantly fewer objects to anchor them. If there is to be a substantial amount of fast camera movement, as there is in *The Slender Thread*, then the audience will necessarily become a part of it. While such techniques work well for Cinerama, where the application is both intentional and expected, they did not work well for *The Slender Thread*. In responding to a question about the camera movement in this film, Pollack suggested from a retrospective of twelve years of experience in directing films that the audiences would be well advised to take Dramamine before watching it.

Although limitations are placed on a new film director, the parallels in camera movement, as well as the use of music and the film's structure (to be examined in the next chapter), which exist between *The Slender Thread* and Pollack's work in television speak of his early strength in the film industry. While such strength cannot be measured in terms of financial control, as in Pollack's later films when he was both the director and the producer, it can be measured in terms of the respect afforded to him by members of the production team.

Pollack's winning an Emmy for the television production of "The Game" on the Bob Hope "Chrysler Theatre" and his being an individual who combined perceptiveness with the necessary fluency for conveying his ideas seem probable justifications for attributing a film like *The Slender Thread* to him rather than to the producer, cinematographer, production designer, or other members of the film unit. Film *is* a cooperative venture, but when an early film like *The Slender Thread* bears marked similarities not only to Pollack's past work in television but also to the 1977 production of *Bobby Deerfield*, the logical assumption is that the director of both contributed a significant amount of his thinking in all areas of the films. No other member of the production team for *The Slender Thread* also worked on *Bobby Deerfield* with Pollack.

Following Pollack's work on this first film, Redford was cast, in 1966, in *This Property Is Condemned*. Natalie Wood, the star of the film, had director approval. Pollack's agents at the time, the William Morris office, took prints of two of Pollack's television shows, "Two Is the Number," and "A Cardinal Act of Mercy," for Miss Wood to screen. After an interview with Pollack she approved him for the job. In *Property* Pollack first worked with Stephen Grimes, a production designer who would work on most of Pollack's later films; Howard Koch, Jr., the second assistant director who would later be the first assistant on *The Way We Were*, and presently a producer; and Bernie Pollack, the costume designer for many of his brother's films.

Following *Property*, Burt Lancaster again contacted Pollack to ask for some help on a couple of scenes from his currently completed film *The Swimmer*, which was directed by Frank Perry. Lancaster and Pollack then collaborated on *The Scalphunters* in 1967 and *Castle Keep* in 1968. These films led to *They Shoot Horses, Don't They?* (1969–70), which brought about a radical change in Pollack's career on an international level.

Pollack notes that "the change was not as drastic as some people think. *Horses* gained some international notoriety, people in Europe began to go back to look at my earlier films, and it generated an interest in my career, but careers in Hollywood are in a state of flux all the time."

Horses was an unusual critical success, but it was not as great a financial success as were other of his films. It received nine Academy Award nominations including Best Direction, and it won an Academy Award for Gig Young. It also won Best Picture and Best Director awards at the Yugoslavian Film Festival, a Special Prize at the Cannes Film Festival, First Prize at the Belgium Film Festival, the Jury Prize at the Moscow Film Festival, and a Director's Guild Nomination for Outstanding Achievement in Film Direction.

After *Horses* Pollack became interested in the possibility of doing *Dirty Harry*. "I thought it a potentially interesting picture, but I wanted to change it radically. I met with the writer, Harry Julian Fink, in Switzerland. He didn't want to change the script. I was wrong. He was right. If *I* had made *Dirty Harry* it probably wouldn't have made a nickel. *Dirty Harry* is what it is; it shouldn't be tampered with." By the time Pollack decided not to do *Dirty Harry*, he had his first look at the script for *Jeremiah Johnson*.

The film, starring Redford, had its world premiere at the Cannes Film Festival, the first Western ever to be invited there, and it went on to receive acclaim as one of the year's ten best from the *Los Angeles*

Times, the *Readers' Digest*, the *New Republic*, and several television reviewers. It also received the Western Heritage Wrangler Award and won the *Parents' Magazine* Special Medal of Merit Award.

Characteristically Pollack began shooting this film, like all his others, without a finished script. As Pollack has stated, "I've never done a picture with a finished script. I'd like once in my life to start a picture with "THE END" written. In *Jeremiah Johnson* I was writing sections of the farewell scene six weeks into the shooting. I was in a motel on a Sunday fiddling with that scene and trying to find the end of the picture."

After the completion of *Jeremiah Johnson* Pollack starred Redford again in his next film, *The Way We Were*, which was completed in 1973. Commercially very successful, the film also received six Academy Award nominations and won two Oscars for music: original score and best song by Marvin Hamlisch, with words by Marilyn and Alan Bergman. The original score of the theme song is framed on the wall in Pollack's office at Burbank Studios.

The commercial success of these previous films was not repeated by *The Yakuza* (1974), filmed in Japan with Robert Mitchum in the starring role. It was shown only briefly in the United States. Rex Reed and Judith Crist were two critics who liked it, but their influence was not strong enough to bring people to a film which made heavy demands on its audiences. Pollack commented about the film, "Both *Castle Keep* and *Yakuza* have their own little cult following in a certain way. Some people who see *The Yakuza* are affected by it; it's run over and over again in one of those Cinémathèques in Paris. It's not a film for everybody any more than *Castle Keep* is. They're both more personal films than some of the others I've done. A career in this country is different from a career in Europe. One has to straddle a couple of different worlds here. We operate in a tight economic system, and you survive by making pictures that survive. What you do is earn the right to do one or two deeply personal films for every hit film you make. So you have to make successes in order to make more personal films.

"You try to make those films as painless as possible. You try to find something that you're sufficiently interested in that you can spend a year working on knowing that it's not on the same level as some of the other pictures that you want to work on.

"Sometimes you hit a nice balance, like in *Jeremiah Johnson*. *Jeremiah Johnson* is a picture which is very personal, but it was also a commercial picture. One of the reasons I've been able to survive, and when I say 'survive' I mean in terms of business in Hollywood, is that my films have been fairly broad-based. Nobody can quite pigeonhole me. They can't quite say, 'He's going to make an artsy film that isn't going to make any money.' I'll do that, too, but I'm liable to make a fifty million dollar grossing picture. Nobody knows.

"You can really make quite interesting personal pictures, but you can't make them for the kind of money that I've spent making studio pictures which are very expensive; four, five, six, ten million dollar pictures. When you make pictures that cost that kind of money, you have to reach a lot of people, you just have to. You don't get it back with limited critical success.

"You achieve a level; a flop doesn't hurt that badly, and a hit doesn't help that much. If you make eight or ten films, and forty percent of them have made money, then you don't go from the basement to the penthouse with an internationally successful film; you vary a couple of floors. Two or three expensive flops in a row puts you in trouble—you would be the fifth, sixth, or seventh to get a script rather than the first or second, but you are constantly affected by how successful your films are commercially. So to get the right to make *The Yakuza*, I must make *The Way We Were*."

After the failure of *The Yakuza*, Pollack selected *Three Days of the Condor* as his next film. Starring Redford and Faye Dunaway, the film is an action thriller about covert governmental actions, and it was released in 1975 in the wake of the Watergate scandal.

Pollack was to travel to Europe in 1976 to film *Bobby Deerfield*, but before starting this highly artistic film, which sent film critics into either paroxysms of joy or despair, he read the preliminary script for *Julia*.

As he explains, "*Julia* was something I very much liked. Richard Roth came to me with the rights to *Julia* while I was doing *Condor*. He already had a commitment from Jane Fonda. Roth had the idea to use Alvin Sargent as the screenwriter, and the three of us spent a week with Lillian Hellman in Martha's Vineyard. I worked with Alvin Sargent on the structure of the screenplay, and I helped talk Lillian into letting us use Dashiel Hammett and Lillian as characters in the film. The short story 'Julia' was for me a jewel which needed a ring to set it in. You could not enlarge 'Julia' without ruining it. What you needed to do was to surround the short story with material that would give it a setting. That material we kept finding in *Unfinished Woman* and *Pentimento*.

Photo: Pollack helps to stabilize balloon during filming of *Bobby Deerfield.* Man at right in shorts is Pollack's brother Bernie; Marthe Keller as Lillian is in gondola.

"Lillian was resistant only because she felt that once Hammett was in the piece, he would overshadow it. She resolved the problem and agreed to permit the use of Hammett as a character.

"In the meantime, Alvin had written *Bobby Deerfield,* so while Alvin was writing *Julia,* I read *Bobby Deerfield* and made a deal to do it. I was in Rome screening actresses for *Deerfield* when the script for *Julia* arrived. I liked it a lot, but I was in a dilemma. I had already committed to *Deerfield,* and I loved it.

"I had a meeting at Fox with Alan Ladd, who needed a start date for *Julia.* I released my right to make the film because I wanted to see it done, and because I had the commitment to *Deerfield,* and [Fred] Zinnemann eventually did the film."

Pollack's most recent film is *The Electric Horseman.* His fifth with Redford, the film also reunites him with Jane Fonda. Pollack also gave Willie Nelson his first screen role in this film and will produce Nelson's next film, *Honeysuckle Rose.*

Now a director for fifteen years, Sydney Pollack has yet to receive the critical acclaim in the United States he receives in Europe. As he comments, "The French especially found some kind of thread that goes through all of the films that I've done, which I'm not even aware of myself. They look at a body of work, and they see what the preoccupations are, and if they find a line that runs through them, then they begin to think in terms of this whole *auteur* theory.

"I don't think that American film directors consciously try to deal only with specific themes and ideas the way a European film director might always deal with the same problem. American film directors tend to be somewhat more diversified, at least in terms of genre and form.

"I'm not an innovator, and never have been. I got into film eventually because I loved film as a kid, and what I loved as a kid was bullshit movies. That's what I loved. I don't want to change the form. What's disappointing to most critics is that if I do *The Yakuza*, they expect it to be Kung Fu, and if it's not King Fu, that irritates them because they feel it violates the form.

"If I do *Condor*, they expect it to be a straightforward action picture. But I tried to find some idea within *Condor* that interested me, that stimulated and challenged me, but still, on the surface, kept it a thriller. It's a thriller, except there's an underbelly of seriousness in it.

"*The Scalphunters* and *Jeremiah Johnson* are not conventional westerns. They are in form, but not in content. Most critics find that confusing. What's exciting to me is to work within the old forms; there's no reason to discard them; they're terrific, gangster pictures, love stories, war films, Westerns, thrillers—whatever you call them—genre films. I'm not interested in finding a new form for film, but I'd like to give the old forms new vitality. The form is a discipline; it's a terrific discipline."

Pollack could have rested between the December 1979 premiere of *Electric Horseman* and the start of *Absence of Malice* by using his mountain retreat in Utah. He has a home near the Redfords, and Claire Pollack, a student of architecture at Sci-Arc in southern California, has designed a solar house for Lola Redford. But he didn't. Pollack once said to a *New York Times* reporter that "concentration is the only real thing that relaxes me. I'm tense. I was tense as a child; I'm tense today 'Tense' is a polite word for 'nervous.'"[1]

2

The Visual Art

" . . . The visual is very carefully done. I work very hard on a way of shooting which, hopefully, you don't notice. It's hours of thought and planning just to design the shot when Jane Fonda gets killed in "Horses." This is almost impossible to do realistically. It doesn't look like much. It goes by in a second, but what went on in order to do it is quite sophisticated"

—Sydney Pollack

* *

The visual aspect of film, the screen image and its composition, is perhaps the least discussed element in any review or critical analysis of film. Critical judgments of Sydney Pollack's films are no exception. Reviews center on such areas as the abilities of the actors, the film's deviation from a book or play, and the pace and clarity of the dialogue. Although these elements are important, the visual element is all-important since it is essentially the distinguishing characteristic of film as art rather than film as an extension of literature or drama.

While the film director is ultimately responsible for the image which appears on the screen, he cannot achieve this end without the cooperation of the entire production unit. Like the director in the theater, he must work with production designers, costume designers, and others who help to create the "look" of the production. Unlike the theater director, though, the film director must also work closely with the cinematographer and editor in creating the desired image.

A director's success in achieving his desired image is contingent upon, as Pollack has said, "career muscle." While logical argument may be the only means through which a young director may achieve his visual goal, his reputation gained from successful films begins to give him the "muscle" which he needs in establishing the set, locations,

Photo: A subjective shot as Joe Bass looks down on the slain Indians in The Scalphunters. *(courtesy of Sydney Pollack)*

lighting, camera angles, costumes, and final cuts in editing which result as the final production of a movie.

Since Pollack was both the director and producer of *The Yakuza* and *Bobby Deerfield*, the assumption is that the visual image is exactly as he wished it; as producer, Pollack had the final say in all areas of the production. His early films like *The Slender Thread*, *This Property Is Condemned*, and *The Scalphunters* were not within his executive control, yet, with some exceptions in *The Slender Thread*, even these early films afford strong visual elements which serve as complements to the theme.

The logical conclusion to be drawn from the visual strength of the early films is that Pollack established a working relationship with the production team; through discussion and logical argument he was able to achieve his desired image. The image as a complement to the thematic concerns of the later films like *Bobby Deerfield* and *The Yakuza* is as strong in *This Property Is Condemned* and *The Scalphunters*.

The working relationship which Pollack has with each and every member of the production crew provides a major reason for the many similarities which run throughout his films. Although he could be dictatorial and so ensure that his wishes would be carried out, Pollack is not. He works with the crew, and the final image appearing on the screen is the result of the respect which the production crew shows for Pollack's technical knowledge, his artistic vision, and for the man himself.

Although constantly working under the pressures of time and daily production costs, Pollack maintains an even disposition, which can only have a positive effect on the people around him. Even with the mass confusion during filming in a thronged Caesar's Palace for *The Electric Horseman*, Pollack was constantly in control. He always had the time to talk with anyone who had a question or observation regardless of their individual "status." He respected the ideas and opinions of the people working with him. The respect which individuals in the production unit in turn showed for Pollack is significant in his attaining the goals which he had for each shot and scene. Typically, he would be moving lights, helping to control the noise of crowds of spectators, checking the image through the camera, and laughing with the actors at intentional jokes in the script or unintentional deviations from the written dialogue. He was not only totally involved and genuinely concerned with the film itself, but also with the people who were a part of the film process as well.

Sydney Pollack's total involvement with every production aspect in all of his films is indicative of his interest in making them his own. While he does not present a visual signature throughout his work, thereby making his films readily identifiable in terms of style, he does convey thematic similarities throughout his work which will be the subject of later chapters in this book.

In looking at the visual element, though, it is perhaps most valid to approach the films in their production sequence. Pollack's composition in the frame, selection of locations, selection of props, and movement of camera are components of his visual supplementation of the themes.

The Slender Thread (1965)

Before looking specifically at the visual aspects of Pollack's first film in terms of their support of the themes, some observations must be made in order to point out this film as a transitional link between Pollack's television past and his more sophisticated later direction of feature-length movies. In particular, his use of music, his movement of the camera, and his organization and timing of the film's sequences demonstrate the ties which Pollack had yet to sever with television.

The television medium makes very specific demands on a director. Maintaining the attention of a less-than-captive audience is one very specific demand. With the television tucked into the corner of a room, with persons walking in and out of the room, and with other distractions common to a home environment, the television demands that a director sustain the interest of his audience with whatever means possible. Music is one of the means.

The difference between Pollack's use of the music of Quincy Jones in *The Slender Thread* and his use of Dave Grusin's music in many of his later films highlights Pollack's maturation as a director of film. While it would be convenient to attribute the selection of Quincy Jones to the producer of *The Slender Thread,* Stephen Alexander, the music is so strongly parallel to Pollack's use of music in television that his acceptance of Jones as part of the production team is likely.

Like the music of the "Dr. Kildare" and "Ben Casey" programs, the music of *The Slender Thread* is all important in forwarding the mood of the film and in sustaining audience interest. Rather than being of secondary importance to the themes and images, it is important in its own right. The difference between music in television and in film is the difference between music for creating mood and music *to supplement a mood* which has been established through the dialogue and the

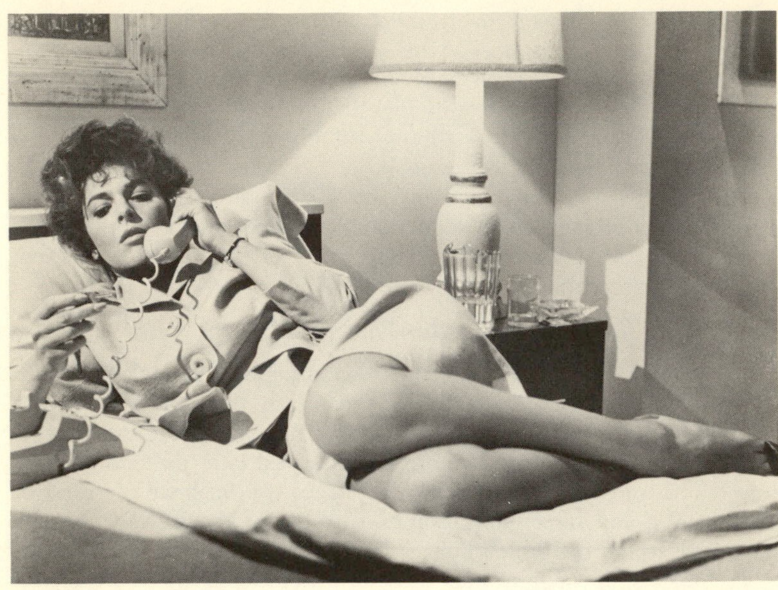

Photo: Inga Dyson (Anne Bancroft) as she talks to the Crisis Center. *(credit: Movie Star News)*

visual art. Since the image on the television screen is necessarily small and, therefore, ineffective in transmitting thematic implications, the music used in television can compensate by, in effect, "telling" the audience what they should be feeling.

Quincy Jones's music in *The Slender Thread* "tells" rather than supplements. While similar in its pervasiveness to the title song of a later Pollack film, *The Way We Were,* it goes even further in that it cannot go unnoticed. Not only loud and not only a part of the background, the music becomes an important transitional link between the scenes.

The volume of Jones's music in *The Slender Thread* is directly related to Pollack's past work in television. In an environment which contains few extraneous sounds, any music used in film draws more attention to itself than that which is transmitted through a small television speaker. Television must compete with the sounds which surround it, and individuals control the television sound while they cannot adjust the volume of the film soundtrack.

In addition to music, Pollack's early camera movement is also indicative of his television past. While helicopter shots are characteristic of much of Pollack's work in film, the helicopter shot in *The Slender Thread* in which the camera takes the viewer from the ground up into the air is difficult for a captive audience to bear. With the film projected onto a large screen which restricts the number of inanimate objects in the field of vision, the audience cannot escape the dizzying heights. Pollack establishes Inga Dyson's (Anne Bancroft) insignificance when the shot of her quickly moves from the ground level to several hundred feet in the air, but he has also inadvertently drawn attention to the camera itself.

In a similar obtrusive camera movement later in the film, the emphasis also falls on the camera instead of on the character. When Inga and her husband, Mark (Steven Hill), go to a discotheque, Inga becomes one with the music and its rhythm while Mark is more passive about the whole environment. Inga's state of mind is necessarily erratic at this point; Mark has recently learned by accident that he is not the father of the boy he thought to be Inga's and his. Inga watches the dancers in her—and their—frenzy, but then Pollack switches to an implied subjective shot which pulsates rapidly as it zooms in and out with the music. Such camera movement is obtrusive enough on a small television screen, but it is overwhelming on the huge movie screen, which provides little visual escape for its audience.

Since the viewer's ease of escape must be a major consideration in planning television shows, with their frequent commercials and less than sedentary audience, the structure which television productions take is directly related to this situation. Television hours are entities in themselves, but they are also very much a sum of their between-the-commercials units which must individually reach some sort of climactic high before being interrupted by the commercial break. Audience interest is to be maintained through the interrelationship of the smaller viewing entities. The structure of *The Slender Thread* is similar to a long television show.

Structurally, the film begins with a flashback that precedes Inga's call for help to the Crisis Center after she has taken an overdose of barbiturates. The movie then recounts the significant fragments of Inga's life which brought her to the brink of death. The stability for the film, and for Inga herself, is found in the scenes shot in the Crisis Center as Alan Newell (Sidney Poitier) tries desperately to identify Inga's location.

In keeping with a structural organization directly parallel to his work in television, Sydney Pollack breaks the ninety-seven-minute movie into more than thirty segments. Each presents a fragment with

Inga in the present as he speaks to her from the Center; yet each segment also builds to a climax which implicitly requests that the audience "stay tuned." While the film audience is not likely to leave, having paid the price of admission, a television audience would be encouraged to remain so that they could see the fragments become one in the completion of the complicated puzzle of Alan's attempt to locate Inga before she lapses into a coma.

In spite of the many links which *The Slender Thread* has with television productions, it yet offers many illustrations of visual excellence which Pollack has carefully provided so that the image on the screen serves as a complement to the themes. Suggested by a story in *Life* magazine by Shana Alexander, the film presents Inga's call to the Crisis Center as the "slender thread" not only to her life, but also to Alan Newell at the Center. Alan's relationship to Inga and Inga's isolation and anonymity are additional themes which Pollack presents through the image on the screen as well as through the dialogue.

While few of the "threads" shown in the film are obtrusive, it is difficult not to assimilate at least subconsciously the many which are a part of the content of the frames. Mark's large boat, *Provider II,* is tied to the dock with lines, heavy lights hang in the Crisis Center by electrical cords rather than by chains, and a thin telephone line provides the only means which Alan has to save Inga's life. The telephone is ever present, but when Alan talks with Inga and has the cord wound around his neck, Pollack is visually explaining the relationship between the two—a relationship in which Inga holds all of the power.

Inga's visual dominance over Alan is established very early in the film. As Alan drives from the university campus to the Crisis Center, Inga's car travels over a bridge at precisely the same moment that Alan is going under it. The timing of such a shot is much more than coincidental. Alan's relationship to Inga is also shown early in the film as he begins a sketch of the anonymous caller—a sketch which he is unable to complete since Inga is careful not to reveal too much about herself. In yet another shot which "tells" while the dialogue "says," Alan is pictured in the frame at such an angle from the camera that the loudspeaker box in the Center is seen above his head. Since the speaker provides Alan's only sense of Inga as a person, Pollack is essentially saying that Inga maintains the dominant position.

The speaker box also reinforces the anonymity of Inga's character while forwarding the sense of entrapment which has brought her to the brink of suicide. Inga is but a voice confined in a small box. Further visual evidence of Inga's anonymous nature is pictured in the plastic flower which she has attached to her car aerial. Shown in close-up, and shown randomly throughout the film, the flower is a tangible representation of Inga's lot in life. With thousands of other flowers stamped out in exactly the same form, the plastic flower is the epitome of Inga's feelings of worthlessness, of a plasticity which negates any warm response.

Although the film ends on a somewhat optimistic note with the rescue of Inga only seconds before she is to die, the anonymity remains. Alan could have taken the opportunity to meet her, but, as with the unfinished sketch which he started when he first talked with her, he chooses not to fill in the unknown features. The warm bond of friendship which was established between the two of them is to be severed, and the thread is to be cut like the dissolution of male/female relationships in Pollack's other films. The dialogue of the film has said it, but the image on the screen lets the audience see it as well.

This Property Is Condemned (1966)

Although only one year elapsed since the release of *The Slender Thread*, the premiere of *This Property Is Condemned* in 1966 illustrates a significant artistic growth in Sydney Pollack's career as a director of film. Edith Head continues as the fashion designer in *Property* as she did in *The Slender Thread*, but the clothing in the later release has greater thematic significance. Loyal Griggs has been replaced by James Wong Howe as cinematographer, but so many strong parallels in camera work exist in *Property* and Pollack's later film of the Depression, *They Shoot Horses, Don't They?* that we cannot negate the impact that Pollack had on the filming of both. Music, a third means of comparison, has also become more closely aligned to thematic matters than it was in the earlier film.

Like the title song in *The Way We Were*, "Wish Me a Rainbow" of *This Property Is Condemned* is an integral part of the theme of the film. Set in the Depression, *This Property Is Condemned* is the story of the Starr family. Mrs. Starr (Kate Reid), deserted by her husband and left with her two daughters, Alva (Natalie Wood) and Willie (Mary Badham), runs a broken-down boarding house in Dodson, a southern railroad town. Owen Legate's (Robert Redford) entrance into town as a hatchetman for the railroad provides one possible escape for Alva in her desperate attempt to break away from her mother. As the more beautiful daughter of the two, Alva is in effect condemned by

Photo: Pollack in helicopter checks the image of Willie Starr (Mary Badham) wearing the remnants of Alva's clothes. *(courtesy of Sydney Pollack)*

her mother as her means for financial security. Willie, an awkward and plain adolescent, is yet another property which is condemned.

Escape from the grasp of the Depression is everything to the Starr family. The song "Wish Me a Rainbow" is appropriately used throughout the film, for the lyrics speak of the film itself. The pace of the song, and the variation given to the pace of the song, further intensify its function in the film. Set in an environment in which individuals drink themselves into a stupor as their means of escape, the song is lively. It is uplifting; it carries the audience as well as Willie and Alva out of the dreary routine of their rather sordid lives. While the music of Quincy Jones had little actual effect on the characters of *The Slender Thread* but served only in the creation of the mood for the audience, "Wish Me a Rainbow" is an integral part of *This Property Is Condemned.* While it does create a mood for the audience, it creates a mood within the characters themselves as well.

Willie sings the song in the beginning of the film while dressed in the tattered remains of Alva's clothing. The film is Willie's story as she recalls the period immediately preceding Owen Legate's coming to Dodson. The clothes and jewelry which Willie wears are all that remain of Alva. The jewelry may remain intact, but the red dress is in shreds. When Alva wore the dress, it dominated the frame through the brightness of its color in a world of more earthen tones and through its clinging to Alva's body. When Willie wears the dress after Alva's death, the color is subdued by grime and tears which proclaim both its appropriateness for Willie and the difference between the two sisters. With a boy's name and an undeveloped figure, Willie is a pathetic representation of the futility of attempted escape in the closed world of the Depression.

Willie's wearing a grown-up dress while still clutching a childlike doll illustrates her position between two worlds. The particular doll which she grasps further visually symbolizes Willie's role in life; while the top half of the doll is from a once-elegant china doll, the bottom half is clearly that of a Raggedy Ann with the red stripes on its legs. Such is Willie's position in life at the end of the film as she walks away from the railroad siding and onto the tracks of the main line.

A smoothly climbing helicopter shot at the end of the film takes us from our intimacy with Willie to a much grander view of the world. In opening the frame with a view of the sky, Pollack is giving both us and the characters the space which has been denied through the entrapment of the Depression which we have shared with the characters. The feeling of confinement which has been so much a part of *This Property Is Condemned* has a marked reflection in the later Depression film, *They Shoot Horses, Don't They?* because it speaks visually of individuals who are trapped within their environment.

With entrapment as one of the themes, Pollack chooses to film many of the scenes at night or within the confines of four walls. Because of the presence of tangible walls in most scenes or because of our inability to see into the darkness in other scenes, we are constantly made aware that space is finite. The few scenes in which Pollack does let us see the sky are effective because they are visual complements of characters' tentative escapes from their surrounding realities.

In one exemplary scene, Legate and Willie first walk under store awnings as they proceed down a street. Tangible, finite boundaries surround them. In a significant change of camera angle, though, the frame is opened so that we see the sky after Legate has eloquently mashed an ice-cream cone into the face of one of the boys who has been taunting Willie. Such action is a most tentative escape for Willie, but it is nevertheless representative of a certain freedom which she has not felt previously.

In another shot which is particularly beautiful in its smoothness and fluidity—a shot which Pollack notes as the first such use of a helicopter—the camera takes us from a close-up of Alva in a moving railroad car until we are high above the train, all the while moving in an almost complete circle. Alva is traveling to New Orleans to seek Legate; she has broken the bonds which have tied her to Dodson and to her mother. Both the blue sky and Alva's escape are real. Significantly, Alva's train is also crossing a long causeway which also serves as a supplement to the story of Alva's life as she moves from one distinct environment to another.

Other details too numerous to mention in props and selected locations further serve as visual supplements to the themes in the film. One location, though, is a most effective refinement of the walled rooms which are used for most of the film. When Alva finds Legate in New Orleans and then goes to his apartment with him, they enter an apartment which is small and confining. The difference is that it opens onto an inner courtyard which is open to the sky while closed on the sides. Stephen Grimes, the production designer for this film as well as five other Pollack films, noted that the stairs up to Legate's apartment were built for the film. The stairs serve a practical purpose by giving the camera more light and flexibility in filming the scenes, in which the characters come into the inner courtyard of the apartment building, but they also provide a visual statement of a less confining space which is open to the sky at the top of the frame. Though we see more sky in New Orleans than we did in Dodson, it is not always open; darkness sets in, and rain pours down as Alva's mother discovers the location of her daughter.

The Scalphunters (1968)

Sydney Pollack's third film, *The Scalphunters*, offers further evidence of the visual art which serves as a complement to the themes of the film. Set in the mid-1800s in the American West, the film concentrates on the relationship among three groups of people: the Kiowa Indians, the scalphunters, and Joe Bass and Joseph Lee. While the dialogue and action of the film illustrate the differences among these groups, Pollack visually explains their relationships through their levels on the screen. Visually we are made aware of the dominance of one person or group of people over others. Pollack sets the levels through his use of camera angle, the position of individuals on the natural landscape, and Joe Bass's horse, who quickly reduces riders to ground level.

The story of *The Scalphunters* is one of dominance of one group of people over another. Greed provides the motivation for the Kiowas to take Joe Bass's (Burt Lancaster) furs in exchange for Joseph Winthrop Lee (Ossie Davis), a runaway slave with a classical education who has been adopted by the Comanche tribe. The furs are then taken from the Kiowas by the scalphunters led by Jim Howie (Telly Savalas). When Joseph Lee literally falls into the scalphunters' camp, Joe Bass is presented with the dual task of reclaiming both his furs and Joseph Lee.

The inferior position of Joe Bass in the opening of the film is obvious from his being surrounded by Kiowas as he walks his horse by a stream. He has no chance to escape with his furs. Visually, the relative positions of the individuals are explained also, for while both the Kiowas and Bass are on horseback, the Kiowas are on higher ground. As they are about to take the furs, Bass alights from his horse and assumes an even lower position in the frame.

As a captured runaway slave, Joseph Lee is bound; he is completely within the control of the Kiowas. The extent of his inferiority to everyone on the screen is further explained visually through the angle of the camera. Although both Lee and Bass are standing on the ground, Pollack films the scene with a camera angle which consistently places

Photo: A visual statement of the vulnerability of Joe Bass (Burt Lancaster) in *The Scalphunters*. *(courtesy of Sydney Pollack)*

Bass's head higher in the frame than Lee's. Such definition of the relative position of characters is further carried out when Lee rides the horse while Bass walks. Although such a situation would seem to imply that Lee would have visual dominance over Bass, Pollack continues to use a camera angle which visually stresses the dominance which Bass has over Lee.

The growing bond between Joe Bass and Joseph Lee is of the greatest importance throughout the film. While *The Scalphunters* tells the story of the atrocities perpetrated on the Indians by the white men, it also tells a more important story about the coming together of Joe Bass and Joseph Lee—two men who come together from opposite ends of the American spectrum in a personification of the early spirit of America.

Visually we have seen early in the film that the slave is inferior. The same representation of Joseph Lee is further illustrated when he falls down a hill into the scalphunters' camp while Joe Bass maintains his vantage point on the edge of the cliff—a high vantage point which he consistently maintains while following the movement of the scalphunters. As Joseph Lee slowly brings himself into a position of greater importance with the scalphunters, he also moves toward a position of dominance over Joe Bass. Should the audience have any doubts about the change in the relationship between Bass and Lee, Pollack offers one particularly humorous scene as an explanation of the altered relationship. Bass has slyly moved into the scalphunters' camp at night in order to talk with Lee and perhaps to retrieve his furs. Lying prone in water with a reed in his mouth for air, Bass abruptly rises to greet Lee when he comes down to the river for water. Lee's dominance is stated visually through his holding the upper portion of the frame, but his pushing Bass underwater at the possibility of his detection even more graphically illustrates the change in the relationship between the two men.

The end of the film offers the final resolution of the movement to equality between the two. In a mock battle to end all battles between them, they drop down into a mud hole which is at a lower level than the surrounding ground. When they arise, they do so with the same mud-colored skin. Joe Bass then rises up on his horse above Lee, but he extends his hand to us and to Lee and then pulls him up onto the same level with him. Lee may ride behind, but visually he and Bass are on the same level. Such equality is predictable, for Pollack's comic use of Bass's horse has already explained it. While the horse threw Lee on the command of Bass's whistle early in the film, the horse also brought Bass to the same grounded position on Lee's similar command later in the film.

Perhaps the greatest leveler of them all, though, is whiskey. It reduced the Kiowas to such a state that they groveled about their camp and were truly vulnerable to the marauding scalphunters riding in on horseback. With slowed reflexes the Kiowas are ready targets. Their reduced state is shown clearly on the screen when one Kiowa attempts to climb up out of the massacre. He is quickly brought back to the level of his other tribesmen by a scalphunter who holds dominance not only in the strength of his rifle but in the clarity of his perceptions as well.

The whiskey-drinking of the scalphunters themselves also brings them to a lower position which allows Bass an opportunity to escape with the furs. The dominance is different in this situation as are the levels of individuals appearing on the screen. While in the former scene a mass of scalphunters on horseback attacked many drunken Indians lying about the ground in their inebriated state, the latter scene presents Joe Bass pitted against the drinking scalphunters who have the additional foresight to maintain a sober watchman. In such a situation, Bass does not hold the position of strength; appropriately, he covers his face with the mud of the earth and crawls among the horses in his attempt to retrieve his furs. He may rise up in order to make his escape, but the futility of his attempt has already been stated visually through his position on the screen.

Whiskey not only provides a certain leveling of groups of individuals, but it also further illustrates a level of the white man's masculinity. Not until the end of the film does Joseph Lee join Joe Bass in drinking. Like Bass, Lee takes the bottle and spits out the cork after he has killed Jim Howie, but it is not until Bass hands the bottle to Lee after their fight that we know that both acknowledge that they are on the same level of existence.

Clearly, Pollack establishes the relative positions of the strength of his characters through his placement of them on higher ground, his use of horses as "levelers," his use of drinking as a symbol of strength or weakness, and his use of camera angles as a means for the visual dominance of a character. One shot near the end of the film may provide the definitive evidence of Pollack's use of visual dominance as an indication of the outcome of a confrontation.

Although a scalphunter is presumed to be dead, Jim Howie arises from his "grave" in order to launch the final attack on Bass. Appropriately, Pollack uses a ground-level camera angle so that Howie appears at the bottom of the frame, Bass in the middle, and Lee at the top. Although Lee (as the cultured and more passive Easterner) would apparently hold the weakest position in this confrontation because of his naiveté about fighting, his eventual killing of Howie while Bass remains tied has already been stated visually. We have been provided with Joseph Lee's dominance and strength in this situation as we have been provided with visual statements throughout the film which have reinforced the levels of strength of other characters.

Castle Keep (1969)

Although we again see Burt Lancaster riding a horse in *Castle Keep* as he did in *The Scalphunters*, and although the visual aspect of the film continues to speak of the dominance which individuals have over each other, the central theme of the film is not the same. *Castle Keep* speaks of fighting for a principle, but more importantly, it speaks of the contrasting values of the Europeans and the fighting Americans. In visually supplementing the differences between the cultured Europeans and the fighting spirit of the Americans, Pollack offers an image on the screen which continually makes us aware of the differences in attitude between the two cultures.

Of the films which Pollack has directed up to the present, not one has more to say visually than *Castle Keep*. All films tell stories and create realities for their audiences, but *Castle Keep* creates a story within a story. Private Benjamin's (Al Freeman, Jr.) narration in the beginning of the film starts with "Once upon a time . . . ," so we as an audience are never to know whether the image on the screen is a recreation of fact or fiction. Pollack uses several techniques throughout the film: an emphasis on perception, short siding, and questionable actions from characters in order to maintain indecisive reality throughout.

The central story line of the film is straightforward. During World War II, a unit of American soldiers led by Major Falconer (Burt Lancaster) moves into the Belgian castle of the Comte de Maldorais (Jean-Pierre Aumont) in an attempt to save it from the Germans. By the end of the film, the castle and the American soldiers, with the exception of Private Benjamin, are destroyed.

Early in the film, we as an audience must struggle to see. The camera brings the windshield of a jeep to the center of the screen; the men

Photo: Vague perceptions characterize *Castle Keep* as Capt. Beckman (Patrick O'Neal) and Sgt. Rossi (Peter Falk) helps push Maj. Falconer's (Burt Lancaster) jeep. *(courtesy of Columbia Pictures)*

behind it speak, but the windshield is so dirty from the mud and grime of the soldiers' journey that we can barely see the men speaking behind it. Similar problems with our perceptions exist later in the film with the hazy red lighting of the Red Queen brothel, the white glare of snow-covered areas, the fog of early morning at the castle, and the smoke of battle. We see, but we don't see everything clearly. Pollack stresses the atmosphere to the diminution of character in the way that a dream would also intensify the atmosphere. Even the speed of the camera helps to forward the notion of the film as a dream. While Pollack makes sparing use of slow motion in his films, he uses it throughout *Castle Keep* as a component in the creation of an other-worldly atmosphere.

As a further visual statement about perception, Pollack uses three characters who are unable to see with both eyes: Major Falconer, with the patch over one eye, Corporal Clearboy, (Scott Wilson) who near death loses his vision in one eye, and as Sargeant Rossi, Peter Falk, an actor with the use of only one eye. It seems more than coincidental that three of the major characters have limited vision and that many of their perceptions become audience perceptions as well through Pollack's use of subjective camera shots.

Our perceptions of the images on the screen are also made dreamlike by Pollack's use of short siding. It is an unobtrusive means of adjusting reality. When characters speak in most films, they usually speak toward the remaining open space of the frame. With short siding, they speak to the edge of the frame, as if to no one, with the open space behind them. Individuals watching the film would not be able to explain their uneasiness about the film, but short siding makes them feel something different from what they normally would feel if the film did not use this technique.

Similarly, Pollack also creates a dreamlike state through his use of lighting. Instead of lighting the side of a face nearest the source of light, he has lighted the opposite side. Again, the audience would not likely notice the technique even though it was affecting them. Neither short siding nor reverse lighting is readily apparent to a general audience, but both provide a disturbing element to the reality of the image on the screen and so promote the film's questioning of reality.

Other elements in the film also distort reality as we know it. Without the recognition of the film's overall dreamlike state, an audience might think such elements absurd. For example, Corporal Clearboy seems the most unclear of all of the characters in his working apart from reality as we know it. He cannot swim, yet he survives a forty-foot plummet into the castle moat, climbs into his floating Volkswagen, starts it, and drives out of the moat. He also avoids the Red Queen brothel, but he stares at a painting of a sensual woman until she comes to life before him. In a fast cut which many in the audience could miss, he is even caught kissing a statue. Additional situations of this order occur throughout the film, but rather than complicating the film, they reinforce the dream-like atmosphere of the entire film.

As in all of Pollack's films, *Castle Keep* contains props which will enhance the themes of the films without being obtrusive. The griffins which guard the entrance to the castle provide an illustration of this point.

A symbol out of mythology carved out of stone, the griffin endures longer than any of the other sculptures which surround the castle. As a mythical animal, the griffin has the hind legs of a lion and the head and wings of an eagle. Such form combines the art of the past, which the Comte de Maldorais is trying to preserve, with the eagle representation of America, the agent of the destruction of the castle and its art treasures. When one of the griffins is blown apart by German mortar fire, Pollack cuts to a very fast image of blood coming from the shattered statue. This image not only illustrates the destruction which the Americans have brought to the castle through their efforts to defend it, but it also points out the destruction of the art treasures which Captain Beckman (Patrick O'Neal) had so carefully tried to preserve.

Several other props in *Castle Keep* are also used to reflect the American soldiers' presence in the ancient castle, but the image of the keep itself dramatically contrasts the American unit with the old European past. After climbing to the keep while still dressed in their muddy, drab fatigues, the soldiers mutter about elevators, flush toilets, and the presence of blacks in the neighborhood. As they speak, they partially obscure a beautifully luxuriant fresco which had been painted on the wall in some past century. They are as out of place here as they have been when using bottles of aged wine as bowling pins, and when Rossi commented that Reubens's *Connubial Chase* must have been painted during his "horny period."

Castle Keep remains as one of Pollack's most obscure films in the United States most likely because of the importance of the audience's understanding of the visual element in order to gain complete understanding of the film itself. The film does not operate well on an action-thriller level; it is not simply a war story, but neither the narrator nor the action tells us this. Visually the film speaks of the futility of war. It shows the inane destruction of life, of art, and of beliefs, but it places it all in a timeless structure much like a nightmare. Like all dreams, reality as we know it provides the foundation, but time is irrelevant as soldiers move from their jeep to the turrets of the castle, and Major Falconer mounts a white horse and rides among the soldiers.

They Shoot Horses, Don't They? (1969)

While *Castle Keep* defies realities as we know them and so conveys the nightmare of war, *They Shoot Horses, Don't They?* presents a living nightmare about the Depression. There is no "Once upon a time" introduction to it; the film allows no escapes for either the audience or the characters in it. Like Pollack's other film of the Depression, *This Property Is Condemned, They Shoot Horses, Don't They?* is a film of entrapment.

With a dance marathon being held at the Pacific Ballroom for a setting, the film concentrates primarily on Gloria (Jane Fonda). She, like the other contestants, has come to the marathon with the hope of winning the promised $1,500 grand prize. Unlike the other contestants, though, Gloria's participation in the marathon teaches her the futility of life itself. She is caught in an endless circle of dehumanizing action until, like an injured animal, she finds death as her escape from pain. The parallel between the contestants and animals is another aspect of the film which is given careful visual attention.

Nothing is made more clear visually by Pollack than the self-imposed entrapment which the contestants undertake in their effort to win the prize. The Pacific Ballroom sits next to the pounding surf and the seemingly infinite boundaries of the ocean, yet the interior of the ballroom itself remains the location for more than 90 percent of the film. With Robert (Michael Sarrazin) we may catch an occasional glimpse of the ocean when a side door is opened briefly, but such openness is severely limited. Even these brief glimpses of the ocean remind us of our more mundane reality, for trash cans line the side of the frame. As in *This Property Is Condemned,* limitless space and its inherent freedom are to be seen only fleetingly. We, like Robert, remain confined in the enclosed ballroom.

Pollack visually tells us of the confinement of the contestants also by filming approximately 98 percent of the movie in either medium or close-up shots. We are not only within a building, but we constantly see people massed together; we rarely have any feeling of freedom. In talking about the film, Pollack parallels his use of the camera for crowd scenes with a cookie cutter—as if it arbitrarily takes a section of a greater whole with a disregard for parts of people which have been cut from the frame.

Pollack does shoot from the ceiling on two or three occasions, but even these shots speak of confinement. The frame remains closed—support beams cut across the top, or the ceiling itself provides the roof for the top of the frame. The lack of openness and freedom in the frame is Pollack's visual statement about the nature of the Depression.

Additionally, the camera speed offers visual detail about the individual's inability to move freely. Slow motion is used primarily for the filming of the derbies, the circular elimination races intended to add excitement for the audience and exhaustion for the contestants. (Pollack himself filmed the derbies while being pushed around the circle on roller skates.) The slow-motion shots of the derbies are particularly graphic in showing the masses of contestants elbowing and trampling

Photo: The claustrophobia of the dance marathon captured visually. *(credit: Museum of Modern Art/Film Stills Archive)*

each other in their frantic attempt not to finish among the last three couples, who will be eliminated

Pollack also shows entrapment in the criminal sense through the flashforwards of Robert's being taken to jail. This kind of entrapment is enhanced visually through the darkness of each jail sequence as it is intercut through the lighted ballroom. Visual clues to the imprisonment sequences are seen at the ballroom. The windows which Rocky (Gig Young), the emcee, sits beside offer no view of the world outside of them, and they also are characterized by heavy vertical bars like those in a cell.

Imprisonment is also implied visually in Rocky's office when he is talking to Robert. Robert stands in front of open venetian blinds. We can see nothing outside, and the shadows of the blinds run across Rocky. The implication here is of Rocky's imprisonment in his situation as well, but it is only a suggestion of his being held rather than a distinct statement.

Although the entrapment and imprisonment of the Depression constitute the primary theme of *They Shoot Horses, Don't They?*, the film also underlines the animalistic condition to which the people have fallen. Reflecting the film's title, the contestants are pictured in situations much like those to be found with animals. At the sound of a bugle call like that of a Kentucky Derby, the contestants run their own derby. Like horses, they eat and sleep while standing. A prominent sign in the ballroom states, "Please Don't Touch the Contestants," with its implied connection to one at a zoo; helpers on the dance floor wear the word "Trainer" on their backs; and the contestants have to grovel for pennies on the floor in the way that an animal might grovel for food.

Gloria's "suicide" with Robert's help at the end of the film is shocking, but Pollack has very carefully explained her motivation through the dialogue, through props, and through the composition of the frame. Reduced to an animalistic state with no means for escape, she had little choice.

Jeremiah Johnson (1972)

After filming the claustrophobic world of a dance marathon in *They Shoot Horses, Don't They?*, Pollack moves his cameras outside, shooting *Jeremiah Johnson* on location in Utah. In some ways, though, *Jeremiah Johnson* is itself claustrophobic despite the mountain wilderness setting since Jeremiah (Robert Redford) is anything but free as he battles against Indians and his environment in his attempt to survive. Pollack at times shows us the panoramic beauty of the mountains, but he also shows us the harshness. Nature also serves in this film as a metaphor for Jeremiah's clarity of vision as he moves into a timeless environment.

Pollack presents nature's dominance over Jeremiah early in the film through action sequences and through the composition of the frame. When in the beginning of the film Jeremiah struggles to catch a fish with his bare hands immersed in an icy brook, we are acutely aware of his vulnerability. Even when he finally succeeds in building a fire, his vulnerability is proven again as the wind shakes the branches overhead and drops snow onto the flames. The forces of nature dominate since Jeremiah lacks the skills required by his new environment.

Visually, Pollack establishes the same dominance of nature by providing a feeling of entrapment through the composition of the frame. As we follow Jeremiah in his struggle to survive, Pollack makes us very much aware of nature's presence. The camera follows Jeremiah in

Photo: Jeremiah Johnson visually integrated into wilderness late in the film. *(courtesy of Sydney Pollack)*

tracking shots, but trees come between us and Jeremiah; they obscure our view as they clearly hold the dominant position in the frame. Overhanging branches of trees further express the dominance and entrapment of nature as Pollack positions them at the top of the frame and over the head of Jeremiah. In spite of all of the open space available in the mountainous West, our view of Jeremiah is restricted to the confines of the wooded areas for most of the film.

On some occasions, Pollack opens the frame so that we do have a greater sense of space. These shots and scenes are directly related to the freedom which Jeremiah is experiencing at these times. One of our first views of openness comes after Jeremiah has met Griz (Will Geer). Given instruction in hunting and general wilderness survival, Jeremiah is gaining a freedom he had not experienced when he first entered the wilderness. As a visual parallel, the camera is pulled back from the two men, but its distance from them is such that nature continues to dominate. The men appear very, very small in the frame as they stand with towering mountains in the background.

As the seasons change, the sense of freedom which Jeremiah feels also changes. Pollack provides for that change visually in the desert scene in which Jeremiah finds Del Gue (Steffan Gierasch) buried up to his head in sand. Jeremiah's newly gained freedom is a startling and ironic contrast to the buried Del Gue. The desert is a sharp contrast to the cold and steep mountain slopes of winter. The flatness of the sands and their lack of any substantial trees or bushes open the frame so that we can see beyond Jeremiah. His restrictions have been lifted, and greater open space appears as a visual indication of his freedom of movement.

Since the film, however, is concerned with Jeremiah's growing attachment to the mountain wilderness, it shows his returning to that environment which remains a world of little space. While Jeremiah's survival skills have increased to a point that he is less restricted by his environment, his conflicts with the Indians lead to a new sense of entrapment through a surprise attack. By the end of the film, though, the position of strength Jeremiah has achieved by surviving the Indian attacks is shown in the composition of the frame. The distance between the camera and Jeremiah has changed from the earlier wide-angle shot of him. By the end, Jeremiah stands on a high point of land; the camera is close to him, and he maintains the dominant position in the frame while we can see beyond to the infinite space behind him.

The same parallel between the space in the frame and Jeremiah's position in life is also seen in the log cabin he builds, which is contrasted with the house which Griz has built for himself. While Jeremiah's cabin is set in a small clearing surrounded by trees, the cabin which Griz has is set on an open slope. The locations of the two houses directly reflect the freedom, or lack of freedom, of their inhabitants. In spite of the ease with which Griz apparently moves through life, though, and in spite of the expertise which Griz displays in the mountain wilderness, his house is destroyed by an avalanche. No man is more powerful than the forces of nature.

Jeremiah's house is also destroyed, in a way, as the result of nature's force—not merely the fire which Jeremiah starts that burns the house to the ground, but the force of nature associated with the Indians' reverence for natural spirits. Jeremiah's violation of the Indians' sacred burial ground results in the Indians' killing of his family and in his subsequent burning of his house. In going against the spirit of the wilderness by disregarding the sanctity of the Indian burial ground, Jeremiah has brought a force upon himself which is as strong as any force in nature.

The power of the spirit is seen in the Indians themselves, but Pollack also expresses the idea again through the composition of the frame. While the cabin is burning, we first see the light reflections of the flames on Jeremiah's face before we realize their source. As the flame intensifies, the image of Jeremiah begins to blur as we look at him through the heat waves of the fire. Pollack alters our perceptions of Jeremiah as a parallel to the changes which are taking place within his character as a result of the slaughter of his family.

For the remainder of the film, many of the images which we see extend beyond the realistic view of Jeremiah's daily existence. Living in a nightmare world of continual surprise attacks from the Indians, Jeremiah's world becomes one in which time has no specificity—it becomes a blur of attacks and surroundings which merge together and so lack the strict definitions of a logical time sequence. Pollack uses dissolves as his visual parallel of Jeremiah's nightmare so that both the horrors of action and the beauty of the surroundings blend together. When the Indian attacks finally do cease, we are as unaware of specific time as Jeremiah is as he and Griz try to guess the month of the year.

All that Pollack has done with nature in *Jeremiah Johnson* directly reflects nature's duality. Like our view of the man Jeremiah finds frozen in the snow, nature both destroys and preserves. Pollack shot a second ending of the film which would have shown Jeremiah in the same frozen position, but Jeremiah has become a living legend. He is not yet a Griz, who with his white horse and white furs is one with the environment, but he wears brown furs and an animal hat which attest to his adaptation to the mountain wilderness.

The Way We Were (1973)

Perhaps the most financially successful film of Pollack's career, *The Way We Were* is also his most straightforward film in the sense that audience expectations are immediately satisfied. We do not question the plausibility of actions and events in *The Way We Were* as we would in *Castle Keep* or *Bobby Deerfield* since Barbra Streisand's character, Katie Morowsky, and Robert Redford's character, Hubbell Gardiner, represent people whom all of us have met. Their interests and sensitivities are like ours, and the world in which they live is one that we recognize easily. Katie Morowsky is a social activist—a strong, domineering woman. Hubbell, in Katie's words, is "America the Beautiful."

With Streisand and Redford cast in these roles, we as an audience are content. They seem perfect for the parts, yet even with these expectations satisfied Pollack goes one step further in his offering of visual complements to the relationship between Katie and Hubbell. The dialogue and action speak of her dominance and the gap which exists between the two people, and Pollack's frame composition offers a visual affirmation of the same.

While the characters' mere presence on the screen immediately shows the unlikely union of Katie and Hubbell, Pollack's presentation of them augments the fact. There is ever a visual space between them, which supplements the distance found in their activities. While Katie is either a speaker, waitress, or server of punch, Hubbell is the listener, customer, or drinker of punch. When Hubbell is the active person involved in such sporting events as jogging, rowing, or racing on a track, Katie is the one who passively watches—usually from afar. Generally, she holds the dominant position in the frame so that she is higher in the frame than he is.

On the occasions when the two of them are participating in the same activity, Katie continues to hold the stronger position. The two of them go out in a boat in Central Park, but Katie rows; they organize their beach house on the West Coast, but Katie stands high on a ladder while

Photo: The visual dominance of Katie Morowsky (Barbra Streisand) over Hubbel Gardiner (Robert Redford). *(credit: Musuem of Modern Art/Film Stills Archive)*

Hubbell sits on the couch. When Hubbell does assert himself on Katie's behalf upon her return from Washington, when he does try to show his strength, he is bloodied.

The only times which Pollack gives Hubbell the dominant frame position are appropriately during Hubbell's performance as "America the Beautiful"—in lovemaking. Katie and Hubbell lie on the floor in her apartment before the requisite romantic fire, and Hubbell almost obliterates Katie in the frame. Their lovemaking in bed is similarly presented. Katie's nakedness is brief and modest while Hubbell's flesh lingers on the screen for Katie's, and the audience's, contemplation of it.

With the love scenes as exceptions, Katie and Hubbell exist at a distance from each other throughout their lives together. Pollack consistently places barriers or space between them as a visual indication of their separateness, or he positions them so that Hubbell is seen with the masses while Katie is seen with the few.

As a leader in the Communist League, Katie speaks from a platform above a crowd containing Hubbell. At a formal dance, Katie is behind a serving table while Hubbell mingles with all of the other dancers. Appropriately, he does not move toward Katie until she is first brought out onto the dance floor. Near the beginning of the film the restaurant in which Katie works shows the separation also as Katie stands alone behind the counter while Hubbell walks in with his friends. Their writing class in college further illustrates the space between them as Hubbell sits with the others in the class when Katie arrives late. Even then, she sits three rows behind him. J.J.'s apartment later in the film continues to show the separation as we see Katie alone in one room while Hubbell converses with his friends in another.

When the two of them are pictured together in the same frame, they are kept visually apart by Pollack's use of such things as tables, streets, or glass. Katie must cross a street to talk with Hubbell as he sits at an outdoor café, but even then he sits behind a stone wall, a light pole, and flowers; all these objects speak visually of their separation. When Katie later works for a radio station, and is suitably in the control room, Hubbell is on the other side of the glass, unable to communicate until Katie flips the appropriate switch.

Their separation and differences are perhaps best shown in their unexpected reunion in New York City. Hubbell emerges from a taxi in front of the Plaza Hotel while Katie distributes leaflets on the other side of the street. They meet and converse, but Hubbell returns to the Plaza side while Katie remains on the opposite side of the street. Interestingly, Hubbell has difficulty crossing the street—he must dodge the traffic when he moves toward the Plaza and its representative life-style. Katie also crosses, but ever in control, she moves with ease through the traffic.

All of the visual supplementation of the differences between Katie and Hubbell have complemented the dialogue and very appearance of the two main characters, but Pollack also furnishes visual information which has not necessarily been provided through the script. Although unspoken, we have been given a visual connection among Hubbell, Katie, and children. When the drunken Hubbell first goes to Katie's apartment they stand on a stair landing first with a tricycle behind them and later with a baby carriage in the background. Street scenes outside of Katie's apartment show children in the background as the couple speak. Appropriately, though, the tricycle sits silently on the landing, and the baby carriage is empty as a visual parallel to their child, Rachel, who remains unseen throughout the film.

As opposed to the visual in a film like *Castle Keep*, the visual aspect of *The Way We Were* is not essential for our complete understanding of the film even though Pollack continues to give it his careful attention. We may well know through Hubbell's actions that he is a sort of cardboard cutout of a man who lacks direction in life as he moves along with others, yet the screen image summarizes his character as we see him sailing aimlessly in a boat with J.J. (Bradford Dillman); the winds and the tides dictate their course as the rudder remains untouched by either man.

The Yakuza (1974)

The Yakuza. Loved by serious film audiences. Scorned by critics. Seen by few. Such is the nature of the film industry in the United States, and such is the response given to, in my estimation, Sydney Pollack's greatest achievement in film to the present.

The failure of *The Yakuza* is to be found in the very definition of its purpose. Although offering scenes of the martial arts, and although casting Takakura Ken, a Japanese actor who has starred in more than 150 Kung Fu films in Japan, in a lead role, *Yakuza* is not simply a film of the Kung Fu genre. The major theme of the film, and the thrust shown through Pollack's composition of the frame, centers on the joining of East and West. A viewer who expects to see an exposition of Kung Fu techniques as the central purpose of the film is disappointed.

A group of Japanese gangsters provide the title for the film. The word *yakuza* is formed from the numbers 8, 9, and 3 in the Japanese language. These numbers equal 20, which, in Japanese gambling, is a losing number. Out of perverse pride, the group uses this name to identify themselves. Characterized by ornate tattoos on the upper half of their bodies (see accompanying still), the yakuza organized themselves over 300 years ago in Japan, where they served first as protectors of the poor, who were being terrorized by noblemen. The group has now evolved into gangsters and con-men who practice their exploits while maintaining very strict codes of honor within their organization.

The complex story of the film unfolds mostly in Japan. Harry Kilmer (Robert Mitchum) is asked by George Tanner (Brian Keith) to help rescue Tanner's daughter, who is being held by the yakuza in Japan because they have not received a shipment of weapons from Tanner which they have already paid for. Kilmer agrees to make his first return trip to Japan since his departure after the American occupation of the country following World War II. At that time, Kilmer had saved

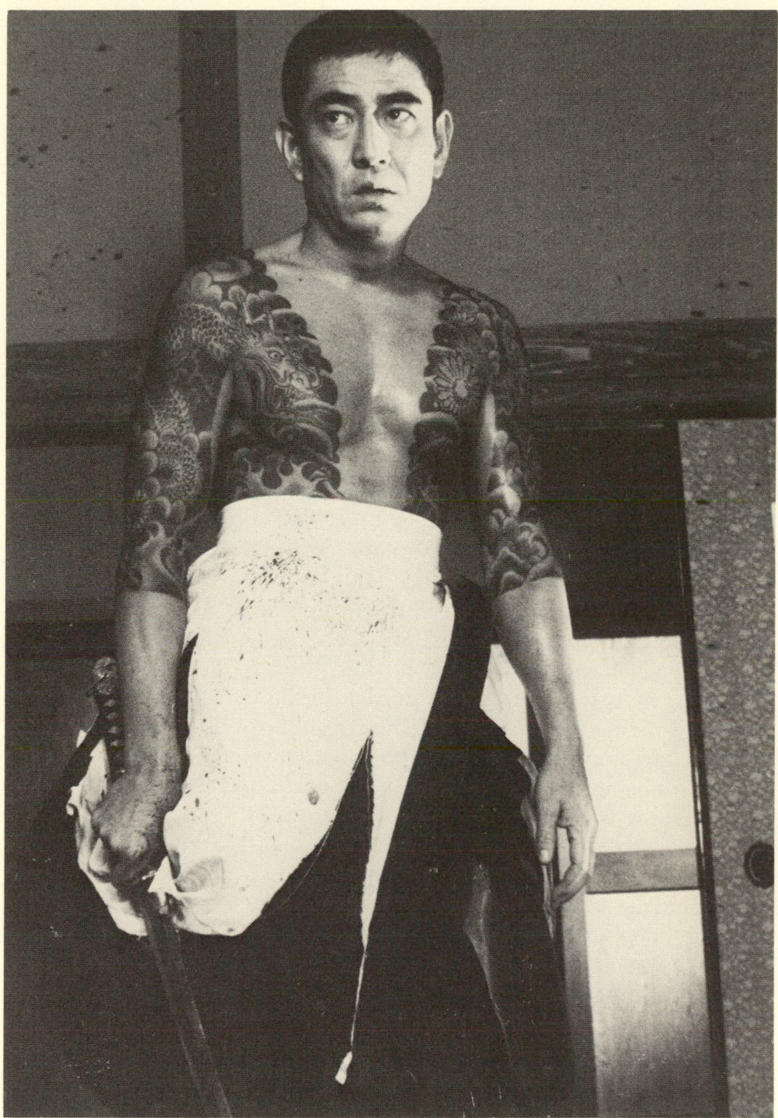

Photo: The intricate tattoos of Tanaka Ken express the strength of his position. *(courtesy of Sydney Pollack)*

Eiko's (Kishi Keiko) daughter, Hanako (Christina Kokuba), from death by providing her with needed medicine. He later lived with them, and through them became friendly with Tanaka Ken (Takakura Ken), a member of the yakuza, whom he believes to be Eiko's brother.

By the time of Kilmer's return to Japan, Tanaka Ken has left the ranks of the yakuza, but because of a feeling of responsibility to Kilmer, he joins the latter in the rescue of Tanner's daughter. Violent battles result in the deaths of many characters, but when Kilmer again leaves Japan he has consciously become as much a part of the Japanese culture as he possibly can through his acceptance of his total responsibility to Eiko and Tanaka Ken. Kilmer learns that Tanaka Ken is actually Eiko's husband, whom she presumed dead when he failed to return immediately after the war. With the death of their daughter as one result of Kilmer's effort to save Tanner's daughter, Kilmer, in the Japanese tradition of *michi*, is doubly obligated to them and so becomes one American who embodies the Japanese tradition through his performance of one of their rituals. Through Kilmer, and through the Americanization of Japan, East and West come closer togther.

Under Pollack's direction the image on the screen continually tells both of Harry Kilmer's part in the Japanese culture and of the American influence in Japan. When in the beginning of the film we see Kilmer's beach house in America, we see a home filled with Japanese objects. Pollack moves one step further, though, in our initial look at Kilmer as he is tending a small garden on his deck facing the Pacific Ocean. Noticing a dying fern, Kilmer recognizes his failure. Then the camera moves until we can see both his flowered deck standing out from the unadorned plainness of other decks and the sterile sands of the beach.

Flowers remain the symbol of Japan, and with Kilmer's presence in Japan we see his assimilation of their culture. When Kilmer first visits Eiko after the years of his absence, he buys her a bunch of flowers in an almost typical American quantitative gesture. Yet, as Kilmer nears the coffee house, in a more suitably Japanese manner he removes a single flower as his gift to Eiko.

The sword as another characteristic of the Japanese culture also provides a means to the understanding of apparently opposite traditions. Even after being warned about the sharpness of the blade of a Japanese sword and about the manner in which such a sword should be respected, Dusty (Richard Jordan) an American associated with Tanner, slashes his hand while toying with one of the swords. As a contrast, Pollack later moves his camera in on an extreme close-up of Tanaka

Ken's handling of his sword as he slides it back into its holder while pushing it through the fingers of his other hand.

As we are provided with further scenes of the Japanese surroundings, we are made more aware of the Americanization, or at least the Westernization, of the country. Wheat (Herb Edelman) lives in a split-level house with high tables and chairs while Tanaka Ken lives in a house with low tables and cushions; still, Wheat's house is filled with ancient Japanese weapons. His Japanese visitors wear Western-style clothing, and a small Japanese garden is seen in his backyard.

Eiko's house also shows the blending of the two traditions. While Pollack does not emphasize the American qualities of her house, we do see American products on the shelves. The neon lights of nearby city streets also proclaim the same duality as they brightly display a mixture of Japanese characters with English letters.

Appropriately, Pollack portrays the greatest compatibility between East and West through the young people of Japan. Their hair is long; they wear blue denim, and while the American Dusty may learn the Japanese tradition of feeling the warmth of his cup before drinking, Hanako will also accept his offer to finish drying the dishes—an act unacceptable for a woman raised in the older tradition who has been taught a position of subservience to men.

As Kilmer remains in Japan, he assumes more of the Japanese ways, and Pollack's camera tells of the relationship which he has strengthened with the Japanese. Near the end of the film, Tanaka Ken's outdoor farewell meeting with Kilmer provides not only our indication of their relationship, but an indication of our relationship to them as well.

Using a camera lens with a long focal length, Pollack separates the American "us" from the Japanese "them." Blurred twigs between them and us help to reinforce the idea, but the long focal length has yet another function. As Kilmer and Tanaka Ken begin to move apart from each other, they seem, from our perspective, hardly to be moving at all. Our perception not only reinforces the established relationship which they share, but also the perception which we continue to have of them.

While many, many additional references can be cited as evidence of Pollack's effective use of the camera, two specific shots seem most appropriate as examples. Both occur near the end of the film, and both speak of Kilmer's position as an American who has come as close as he possibly could in his adoption of Japanese tradition.

Kilmer's act of atonement in severing his finger is in itself Japanese, yet Pollack visually reinforces the idea. The handkerchief containing his finger is white, and as the blood comes through the cloth, it appears in the center. Kilmer's handkerchief becomes the image of the Japanese flag. Tanaka Ken raises it to his forehead, and a drop of Kilmer's blood remains as further evidence of the bond which exists between them.

In spite of the similar repentances which the men have undergone, they can never be the same. Kilmer's leaving Japan implies it, but two important shots show the truth of the men's difference. As they speak together in a room shortly before Kilmer's departure, one shot shows Kilmer by himself with a circular light fixture hanging next to his head. Tanaka Ken is also filmed by himself as the two men speak, but rather than picturing a light hanging by his head, Pollack films the circular reflection of Kilmer's light next to Tanaka Ken's head. In effect, we are given visually the difference between the East and the West. It is a matter of the concrete and the abstract—in a way, like feeling the warmth of the cup before drinking from it.

The story of *The Yakuza* is the story of the blending of two traditions, and such a theme is given the strongest possible visual support by Pollack. If the film were to be a commercial success, then Pollack would have to choreograph additional displays of Kung Fu techniques, blend in further views of the gangster-like activities of the yakuza, and so destroy a film which, like the Japanese themselves, reveres the fragile beauty of a single flower and the solid strength of a sword. Unlike Kilmer's perceptions, a general audience looking at the film concentrates on that which is seen and so loses the feeling for that which is implied or felt . . . looks at the cup, but fails to recognize all that it has to offer.

Three Days of the Condor (1975)

Following the unsuccessful *Yakuza,* Pollack returned to a present-day American setting with his next film, *Three Days of the Condor.* While *Condor* ostensibly has no parallels with his other films set in the United States, it yet contains visual trademarks associated with the theme which help to identify it as Pollack's. As a film which emphasizes governmental intrigue and particularly the entrapment of Joe Turner (Robert Redford) in his attempt to uncover corruption in the CIA, *Condor* has especially visual parallels to Pollack's other films of entrapment: *They Shoot Horses, Don't They?* and *This Property Is Condemned.* Joe Turner in *Condor,* Gloria in *Horses,* and Owen Legate in *Property* all exist in claustrophobic worlds which are detailed through the story line and through the image on the screen.

Turner's world is one of darkness and alleys, and the sophisticated machinery which he uses continually punctuates the film with its dominance over man in the twentieth century.

The story of *Three Days of the Condor* is both complicated and puzzling, but since our perceptions are for the most part those of Turner, we share in his struggle to identify the individuals who have slaughtered all of the people in his intelligence unit of the CIA. Our concerns for Turner's life are intensified, for while he realizes that he is next on the list to be assassinated by some unknown individual, we continually see Joubert (Max Von Sydow) plotting the final murder of his contract. Unable to trust anyone in the CIA, Turner forces a stranger, Kathy Hale (Faye Dunaway), to take him to her apartment. She eventually aids Turner in the discovery of the key men in the CIA who were attempting to make a huge personal profit from their manipulation of world politics.

Our first look at Turner is also our understanding of his position in life. His riding a motor bike in the midst of New York City traffic tells of his vulnerability; the buildings which surround him, as well as the

Photo: Visual barrier used to keep Joe Turner (Robert Redford) essentially apart from Kathy (Faye Dunaway) and Higgins (Cliff Robertson). *(credit: Movie Star News)*

rain clouds overhead, set an atmosphere of darkness which will be a constant throughout the film. Like *They Shoot Horses, Don't They?*, and like *This Property Is Condemned*, *Condor* is a film which shows the entrapment of individuals caught in a position which allows them little means of escape. Rarely is the frame "opened" so that we have some sense of space, but when it is in *Condor*, we see clouds and smoke churning out of huge stacks as well.

Turner's position after running from the scene of the murders in his office is presented visually by Pollack through the use of a phone booth. The use of Panavision with all of its horizontal space makes the showing of confinement and entrapment a problem, but Pollack's use of the telephone booth solves the problem. He sets the booth in the middle of the screen and then sets Turner within it so that he is tightly contained by the booth instead of by the sides of the whole frame. The feeling of confinement is also shown in this shot through the reflections seen on the glass. It is as if Turner is completely surrounded; we have no feeling of any openness or of freedom even when glass serves as a visual reminder of all that surrounds Turner.

Pollack uses glass in other parts of the film as a visual expression of confinement. In Turner's office the glass is frosted so that we can only see the shadows of the individuals on the other side. For the majority of the film, the way that we see people is also their position at that point in the film. For instance, Joubert may be ready to assassinate Turner when he comes out of an apartment building at night with a group of adolescents, but Turner is not be be killed at this point. When we look with Joubert through the telescopic lens of his rifle, we do not see Turner in the small circle of vision; instead, we see a license-plate number which will bring Joubert that much closer to Turner.

Pollack's use of an elevator which the two men share furthers this idea. While a small window on the door could have been used as a visual means to illustrate Turner's almost total entrapment, it was not. Turner has yet some "space." He is undeniably caught in a situation of probable death from our point of view, but Pollack kept the frame partially open as a visual indication of Turner's eventual escape from Joubert. The elevator door opens and shuts while the two men are inside, and Turner still has a means of escape. In fact, Turner even stops the door from closing on three different occasions.

Turner's association with the machines of the 1970s is curious. While they offer in most instances the means to freedom, their presentation on the screen also implies a further dehumanizing quality which speaks of the restrictions upon individual freedoms.

Turner rides a motor bike to work: perfectly acceptable, but then he must dodge traffic; he is not pictured riding in an open environment. Once in his office, he sees on a closed-circuit television that some neighborhood kids are perhaps tampering with his bike, so he must stop his work and go outside to chase them away.

The television monitor itself provides a certain freedom for the secretary so that she can "see through doors" in order to identify the caller without rising. Turner mocks the instrument by hiding his face when the secretary looks at him in the monitor, but she lets him in. She looks again, sees the face of a mailman, lets him in, and is quickly killed.

The freedom granted by the computer in the office also provides a negative side. Turner fixes the machine which opens up a wealth of information to the staff, yet the information which comes from it results in the deaths of the entire staff and Turner's fear for the safety of his own life.

Even the telephone system points out Turner's confinement and lack of personal freedom. Working underground in the confines of the banks of telephone circuits and wires, Turner uses machines to speak to machines. He then makes a mockery of the whole system of sophisticated machinery by linking hundreds of phones together so that the CIA's tracing device will be unable to locate him.

In an audio testimony of the dual nature of machines, Pollack carefully overrides the sound of a machine gun with the sound of the computer printout machine in an implied statement about machines' association with death. The association is not implied in a hospital scene in which we hear the audio amplification of a patient's heartbeat. While we know that the patient is alive, we also have an abrupt indication of the patient's death.

In spite of the efficiency of the impersonal machines, Pollack's use of them also provides a clue to the open-ended character of the film at its completion. When Turner first calls the central office of the CIA, he is directed to leave the receiver dangling. We see it hanging there and are perhaps disturbed by its not being returned to its cradle. When the CIA tries to determine Turner's location with its phone tracer, the screen pinpoints location after location. The device will continue to run until the operator stops it, but Pollack does not allow us the satisfaction of seeing the machine turned off.

One shot of Turner's meeting with Higgins (Cliff Robertson) near the end of the film not only affirms that Turner's life will be in constant danger as long as he remains in the United States, but it also visually reaffirms the troubles which have plagued Turner. Much like the assassin Joubert pulling on his gloves, Higgins performs the same act. He is also standing in front of a restaurant clearly named "McCoy's" as we, with Turner, wonder about the identity of the "real McCoy" who may eventually have Turner murdered. Turner remains unseen by Higgins as he has throughout the film, and scratched in a brick to the left of Turner's head is to the word "Liberty." Liberty will remain his goal until he is trapped.

Turner may have ensured fleeting liberty for the country through his disclosures about CIA activities to the *New York Times;* but Higgins' warning him about his continued vulnerability leaves the door open for the possibility of his being murdered. Pollack provides a similar open-endedness to the film through his use of the Salvation Army singers. They sing "God Rest Ye Merry, Gentlemen," but the image becomes frozen and the soundtrack stops. We are not to hear any mention of "Christ the Savior," since neither we nor Turner have been saved from the future possibility of a similar situation occurring.

Bobby Deerfield (1977)

Of all of the films which Pollack has directed, *Bobby Deerfield* has managed to glean perhaps the widest range of critical response. It has been summarily equated by some to *Love Story* since, after all, the heroine does die of cancer while the hero lives on. Other critics were enthusiastic about the film, for they perhaps saw that the slow pace of it was intentional, that a dull Al Pacino was essential for his role as Deerfield, and that Deerfield's growth in the film was both marginal and magnificent.

Bobby Deerfield, a race-car driver on the Grand Prix circuit, maintains an emotional distance not only from his driving, but from the people who surround him as well. When he journeys to a Swiss hospital to visit a racing colleague who was paralyzed in a crash at the track, Deerfield goes not to inquire about the driver's condition but to determine the cause of the accident. The hospital visit provides a chance encounter with another patient, Lillian (Marthe Keller). At her pleading, Deerfield takes her with him when he leaves for Italy, and their lives become entangled until her eventual death. Like Lillian's fabricated story about her father giving birth through his death, Lillian gives birth to a more vulnerable Bobby Deerfield through her death.

While for the most part the dialogue provides us with the subtle changes in Deerfield's character, Pollack again offers insight through the image on the screen. Deerfield's clothing and occupation provide definitive indications of the man, but, more importantly, Pollack gives

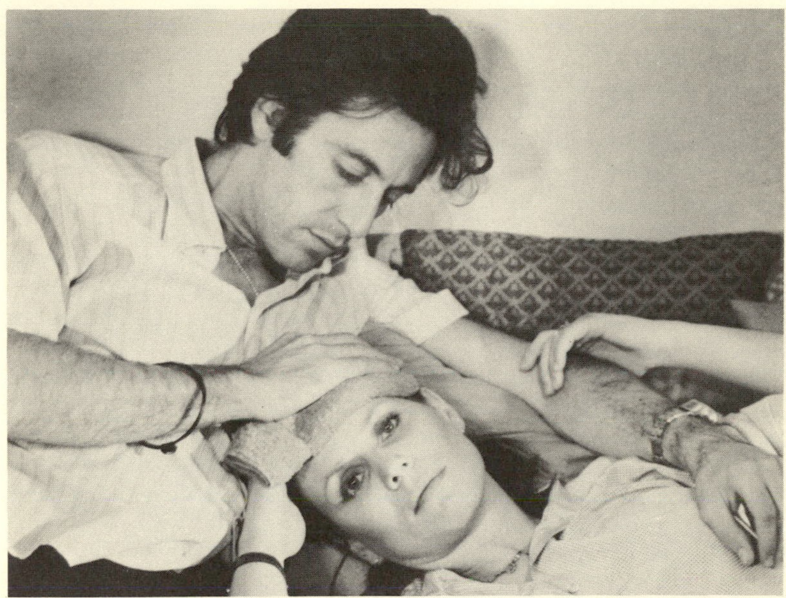

Photo: A depiction of the growing sensitivity between Bobby Deerfield (Al Pacino) and Lillian (Marthe Keller). *(courtesy of Columbia Pictures)*

us visual considerations of the roles of men and women in showing Deerfield's movement toward greater sensitivity and vulnerability. The film tends to equate femininity with sensitivity, and masculinity with insensitivity, so that both the dialogue and the image on the screen use the broad generalizations to show the changes in Deerfield. As Deerfield comes to accept a certain vulnerability, Pollack provides a visual metaphor which eventually shows Deerfield in a most uncharacteristic female impersonation.

Our introduction to Deerfield speaks of the masculinity which is also his protective shield. As he stumbles out of bed, he wears the dog tags of his days in the service. He also wears a watch which through its very size provides further visual identification of Deerfield's image as "a man." The dog tags may symbolize all of the past which he does not wish to recall, but they illustrate more importantly a certain unemotional virility which is to characterize him. Deerfield is the personification of the unemotional soldier who has been trained to do his duty.

His image at the racetrack furthers this idea, for here Deerfield is truly in his element as the calm, rational being who brushes with death for money. His uniform is appropriate. As a visual parallel to his personal protected self, Deerfield wears not only a helmet to protect him from injury, but a flame-proof suit which provides a further means to his invulnerability. Settled snugly in the small cockpit with a protective shield over his eyes, the individual becomes obscured. Such is the character of Bobby Deerfield—a cold and calculating macho race-car driver who is fearless in the face of possible death as he drives onto the track.

The entrance of Lillian at the Swiss hospital provides the visual extreme. Her vulnerability is obvious in our realization that she is a patient in the hospital. As Lillian and Deerfield come together, so the stereotypical masculine and feminine roles fall apart.

One of the first illustrations of the alteration in typical male/female roles is shown in the scene at the bar near the hospital. While our attention may be centered on Deerfield as he sits at the bar talking with the magician, we are also aware of two women dancing together in the background. We do not need to see Deerfield's reaction; the women are merely an early indication of the interchangeability of roles. Individuals need not conform to strict definitions of masculine or feminine behavior.

The dialogue between Lillian and Deerfield on their drive out of Switzerland speaks of male and female roles, for while Deerfield drives the car as he would perhaps drive a race car on the track, Lillian notes that his touch on the steering wheel is "even feminine." In further conversation, Lillian even asks Deerfield about his reaction to the theory that a car is an extension of a man's penis. No comment from Deerfield as he remains personally invulnerable to the possible truth of either of Lillian's statements.

The ride through the tunnel from Switzerland to Italy perhaps best expresses the almost stereotypical role of the two characters at this point in the film. In the privacy of the tunnel's darkness, Lillian first screams and then cries in the full vent of her emotions. Deerfield remains stoic. He is in perfect control, and he does not succumb to this opportunity to display his emotions.

The contrast between the two individuals is further shown in a beautiful ascent of hot-air balloons, yet this sequence performs a double function. It offers a graphic contrast between Lillian and Deerfield, but it also shows a wonderfully acceptable assertive quality to Lillian's character which sets her apart from the stereotypical female role.

Balloons and race cars epitomize the difference between Lillian and Deerfield, and the difference also between a calculated risk and the tangible expression of freedom. Both reach a finish line, but while one traces circles in a machine which is the pinnacle of precision, the other drifts with the wind to a perhaps unexpected destination. The freedom, the aimlessness, which Lillian feels is denied to Bobby Deerfield. Both are in vulnerable positions, but Deerfield is more protected through both his vehicle and his calculated responses.

Lillian's insistence on the balloon adventure, in spite of Deerfield's lack of interest, tells of her refusal to be merely his subservient companion, but Pollack moves one step further visually. In picturing Lillian in the basket of the balloon before the ascent, he moves to a close-up which shows her wearing a cap much like that of a baseball player. On it is written "Markey—For Sportsmen Only." Lillian is not a passive woman who fears dangerous challenges, and the cap proclaims her as one who is comfortable in any situation.

Pollack furthers this idea with Deerfield. He and Lillian row a boat, and they both wear hats. While we have been accustomed to the plastic strength of the racing helmet, we now see him wearing a straw hat which is not without similarities to Lillian's hat. This is not to say that Deerfield has become a different sort of person; it is merely a visual indication of the change which is slowly taking place within him. At this point in their relationship, Deerfield is not relying on his virile, masculine image with Lillian.

The most important change with Deerfield relates to his acceptance of the past. The male/female metaphor continues to provide the means for our understanding of change in Deerfield. While previously he could not even remember the events of his childhood when he was talking with his brother at the airport, he eventually is willing not only to remember, but to perform an imitation of Mae West. The performance is pathetic, intentionally so on Pollack's part, but the changes which Deerfield has undergone in order to be able to do the impersonation are revealed. He selects a female to impersonate, and the act is his acceptance of both a sensitivity and a vulnerability which we have not seen.

The manifestation of Deerfield's step toward his revelation of self is seen in the hospital as Lillian approaches death. In another woefully horrid performance, Deerfield sings, "Boo hoo. You've got me cryin' for you." It is unlike anything which we could have expected from the macho race-car driver seen at the beginning of the film, yet it is only a small step toward his acceptance of his vulnerability as a human being.

With Lillian's death, as with the invented story of her father's death, she gives birth to a Bobby Deerfield who has begun to accept the emotional part of his being. His journey away from the hospital at the end of the film tells of the birth visually, for he moves through the darkness of the tunnel only to exit into the blinding light of day much like the birth of a child.

Like the magic violin seen early in the film which was capable of playing without anyone's help, Deerfield has been performing without the help of anyone else. Even with Lillian's influence in his life, he essentially remains unchanged. Curiously, Lillian's apartment has a violin hanging on one of the walls, and, while pictured near it, she comments that she is not a magician.

Observations about the visual aspect of Pollack's films do not fall neatly into a package which can then be branded "Style" because no identifiable visual techniques run consistently through his films. Similarities which do occur, like the visual entrapment seen in three of the films, are inexorably linked to thematic crossovers—the key to our understanding of Pollack's visual art.

The picture which we see on the screen is the product of Pollack's careful attention to every detail, from camera angle and lens to the props used in the set. The end product is an image which visually supplements the major themes of the film. If the film speaks primarily of a bleak period of time in the history of the United States, then the image will be as bleak and as confining as the dialogue. If the film tells of a growing bond of friendship between two individuals of opposite extremes, then such growing unity will be detailed through camera angles, locations, or the characters' proximity to each other in the frame.

Pollack's "signature" is not to be found in a cohesive visual style, but it can be recognized through the structure of his films and his continual interest in defining an American tradition.

Boys

3

Structured Circularity

" . . . *My films are all circles in some way. I'm never quite satisfied unless the ending has the beginning in it. The characters are different, but they're the same in a curious kind of way because I don't think we as people change a lot. I think we want to. I think we try to, and in some ways we do, but we're never different people*" —Sydney Pollack

* *

The structure of all of Sydney Pollack's films lends credence to the *auteur* theory that the director may be seen as the primary author of his films. Whether we look at Pollack's Westerns, the films of the Depression, or films set in a contemporary time period, we see that all are structured as circles. The circularity is presented through two methods: a manipulation of time through the use of flashbacks so that the beginning of the film is the end, or a more strictly chronological sequence of events and an abstract and existential circularity which shows the main character as being fundamentally the same at the end of the film as he was in the beginning.

Of Pollack's ten films to date, the one with the most complicated structure is *The Slender Thread*, his first. The film first presents Inga Dyson standing by a reflective pool in Seattle, then Alan Newell as he is leaving a college campus. They have no apparent connection until they visually cross each other's paths. After Inga calls into the Crisis Center, where Alan is working as a volunteer, the link of communication is established, and the film then moves into multiple flashbacks which slowly, and perhaps painstakingly, relate the episodes which have brought Inga to the point of suicide. Flashbacks have a parallel to the reality of the film, for Inga's story is unfolding visually for us as

Photo: The contestants race toward the finish line in a derby in They Shoot Horses, Don't They?. *(credit: Museum of Modern Art/Film Stills Archive)*

it unfolds orally for Alan as he listens to Inga on the telephone in the center. We, like Alan, slowly piece together her story.

The further complication of the structure of the film also relates to Alan. In bits and pieces, we see fragments of the furious attempts made by the police and the telephone company to track Inga's location so that they can rescue her before she dies from the overdose of pills.

The film is both appropriate for and reflective of a director who has previously worked as a director in television. The many fragments of the film with their lack of a fluid progression are like segments of any drama made for television. Each scene, whether in flashback or in the present, is a complete unit in itself; commercial interruptions do not alter a fragmented structure which is already present. *The Slender Thread* may lose the urgency of its message when presented on television, but the narrative line is unaltered through commercial interruptions.

The film, like all of Pollack's films, is philosophically a circle. Even in this first film Pollack offers characters who show no fundamental change as a result of the events which we have seen take place in their lives. Inga and Alan will remain as isolated from each other at the end of the film as they were in the beginning. Inga will try once again to sort out her family problems, and Alan will return to his college campus. He chooses not to visit Inga in the hospital when he is given the opportunity to meet her. As they went their separate ways after their paths crossed in the beginning of the film, so they will continue on their separate ways after the end.

The implication here is not that both of the individuals have been unaffected by the communication between them. Instead, Pollack is showing us that neither Inga nor Alan has undergone a fundamental change in character. They are in the end as they were in the beginning of the film. They have completed a circle.

Philosophical circularity continues in Pollack's use of a less complicated structure for four of his films: *The Scalphunters*, *Jeremiah Johnson*, *The Yakuza*, and *Three Days of the Condor*. While these films are like *The Slender Thread* in that they start at the beginning, they proceed in a logical chronological time sequence to the end, and they contain very few flashbacks.

The circularity of these four films is again reflective of individuals who undergo no substantive alteration in character. Events offer insight, but they have no greater effect.

Of the four films, *Jeremiah Johnson* is perhaps the most deliberately structured circle. The persons whom Jeremiah encounters in the beginning are inversely those whom he departs from at the end. After Jeremiah leaves the rugged riverside outpost in order to journey up into the mountains, and as he struggles to survive in the icy wilderness, he first encounters the Crow chief Paints-His-Face-Red. His next meeting is with the mountain man Griz, who, in a wonderfully comic sequence, shows Jeremiah one means to capture a bear by having him chase Jeremiah into the cabin. Jeremiah next meets Del Gue, buried up to his head in sand.

Jeremiah moves on to take a wife and to struggle with the Crow Indians for his intrusion into their sacred burial ground, but as the film nears its conclusion, Jeremiah once again encounters Del Gue, Griz, and Paints-His-Face-Red. The Jeremiah whom we see at the end of the film is a rugged and experienced mountain man rather than the struggling novice who was pictured in the beginning. Yet, Jeremiah has not changed substantially. As a war deserter and loner in the beginning, he continues in his self-imposed isolation at the end of the film. He wears furs rather than machine-made clothing, but the changes which we see are merely superficial.

The sequence of events in *The Scalphunters* does not show the same mirrored reflection of characters of *Jeremiah Johnson*, but it does show the events of Joe Bass's life coming full circle. The film moves in an ordinary progression of time, yet it shows that Joe Bass is at the end as he was in the beginning.

The sequence of Bass's encounters in the beginning of the film closely reflects his encounters at the end. Unlike Jeremiah, though, the lone individual at the onset exits with another at the end; but this difference is an extension of character rather than a change in character.

As a sidenote, the shooting script of *The Scalphunters* calls for an opening sequence showing Bass by himself at his outpost. This sequence was cut in favor of the present opening, which shows Bass by himself for only a short period of time before he meets Two Crows and his tribe at the riverside.

Joe Bass may be pictured alone at the beginning of the film, but his world, unlike Jeremiah's, is not one of isolation. While Paints-His-Face-Red impartially observes Jeremiah's efforts to survive, Two Crows is at once conversant with Bass. In a way, we could say that Bass begins where Jeremiah left off, for Bass is conversant not only with Indian ways, but with their language as well. He is by himself, yet he is very much a part of the people who inhabit the wilderness. Appropriately,

Bass is pictured in a wilderness of heat and warmth. He is one with his environment, unlike Jeremiah, whose presence in the mountains is more of a visual expression of one who is working against nature.

Bass's relationship to his surroundings is important for an understanding of his character and for an understanding of the philosophical circularity of the film. The action of the film indicates its circularity in that Bass is chasing after his stolen furs in the end as he was in the beginning, but that sort of action is not the complete story. We see in Joe Bass an individual who works with others rather than against them. Characteristically, a sense of fair play runs through the film.

The Indians take Bass's furs, but they give him the runaway slave Joseph Lee in exchange. They also take Bass's whiskey, although they later get drunk enough for him to retrieve his furs. Even when the scalphunters slaughter many of the Indians, take the furs, and take Joseph Lee, Bass continues to display attitudes of coexistence rather than destruction. He attempts to take his furs at night without firing a shot; he warns the scalphunters before he shoots or releases landslides, and he gets their horses intoxicated on locoweed rather than killing the riders one by one.

With the idea of coexistence in mind, we can see the end of *The Scalphunters* as a philosophical circle like any other of Pollack's films. It may not seem so on the surface since the individual Bass of the opening of the film rides off with Joseph Lee on his horse at the end, but fundamentally Bass has not changed. He now has a companion—for a time, at least—with him as he goes off again in pursuit of his property, but he has never been one against all others. He is one with his environment in that he makes nature work for him with its natural sewing needles and shampoo, but he is also one with the others around him. His friendship with Lee does not express a radical change in character; it expresses a communication with others which he has always shown.

While *The Scalphunters* follows a logical progression of time without any deviations from strict chronological order, in *The Yakuza* and *Three Days of the Condor* Pollack employs some minor time changes in a generally chronological narrative in order to clarify the story.

Pollack's structuring of time reflects the themes of the films. *The Scalphunters* is the story of a chase; alterations in the sequence of normal events would be confusing. *The Yakuza* is a story about the blending of the old and the new; time itself must be brought to the attention of the audience. *Three Days of the Condor* is a story of intrigue and hazy discovery in which chronology must move logically.

Visually *The Yakuza* maintains a logical time sequence. When we first see Harry Kilmer he is living alone at his California beach house. The many Japanese artifacts throughout his house, and his sensitive concern for flowers and plants, show his connection with the Japanese culture, which is very much a part of his life.

When Kilmer journeys to Japan at George Tanner's request, a significant manipulation of time takes place. We see Kilmer as he walks through the neon city, but as he does, Wheat narrates the story of Kilmer's past connection with Japan and with Eiko. Shortly after Kilmer arrives at the bar which he bought for Eiko, the two of them look at pictures—which we see in full-frame close-up—taken when they were together during the American occupation of Japan after World War II.

In both of these situations, a narration in the present is used to bring different periods of time together. Wheat's narration speaks of the past while the screen image is of the present. In contrast, Eiko and Kilmer's words are of the present while the screen image is of their past together, which we see with them in the old photograph album. The movement of time is both stalled and fused; the span of years between the past and the present is both minimal and mammoth. Narrations not only fuse time in these instances, but they also provide for the fusion of time in the present through Pollack's use of voiceovers in other parts of the film. Like the movement of overlapping waves, the voiceovers take us into a new sequence before we have departed visually from the previous sequence. *The Yakuza* centers on the conflict of the presence of ancient tradition in a contemporary setting, and Pollack focuses our attention on time through his use of narrations and overlapping dialogue in the structure of the film.

The philosophical circularity of *The Yakuza* is like that of Pollack's other films. Although Kilmer renews his friendship with Eiko and Tanaka Ken, and although he is involved in the deaths of many men, he remains fundamentally the same. The Kilmer whom we saw in the beginning of the film, alone and yet a part of the Japanese culture, is the one whom we see at the end as he returns alone to America. He will continue to maintain his connection with the old ways of Japan although he lives apart from them.

Joe Turner also experiences the same sense of isolation at both the beginning and end of *Three Days of the Condor*. He, like Kilmer, shows no fundamental change in character in spite of the horrors which he has experienced in his attempt to uncover intrigue in the Central Intelligence Agency. *Condor*, like Pollack's other films, offers a visual indication of the main character's position in life.

Our first view of Turner shows him riding his motor bike in the midst of New York City traffic. Turner is clearly on his own; he moves with the traffic, but he is more vulnerable than anyone else in the image. Our view of Turner at the end of the film does not alter this conception. The dialogue and action throughout have provided us with the details of his vulnerability, but even as Turner moves into the crowd of singers at the end, he stands out prominently in the middle of them in the center of the frame. He has given his information to the *New York Times* and the carolers are singing about "Christ Our Savior," but Turner remains now as he was before. Philosophically, he has returned to his starting point.

Pollack's use of time in *Three Days of the Condor* is not significantly changed from the straightforward, chronological progression. The only time change is found in Turner's effort to reconstruct the sequence of events in the alley where his friend Sam was set up and killed. The flashback to the alley in Turner's mind is as quick as the rapid pace which characterizes the film. It provides minimal clarification for both Turner and us, and it parallels Turner's and our confusion as we try to uncover the individuals who are trying to assassinate Turner.

Two of Pollack's films, *Bobby Deerfield* and *Castle Keep*, begin with such unspecified positions in time that they emphasize philosophical circularity in that the beginning and end merge into one. *Bobby Deerfield* begins with Deerfield's dream of the race-car circuit before he awakens in his bed, and *Castle Keep* both starts and ends with the words "Once upon a time." The remainder of both films is presented chronologically, yet the openings say everything about lives which have no apparent progressive movement.

Bobby Deerfield's life is, appropriately, the circle of the race track. Although he may increase his efficiency in driving the circuit in progressively faster times, the finish line is both the beginning and the end. The events of Deerfield's life run a similar course, for he seems to live in a world without beginning and end.

His childhood years in New Jersey parallel the opening of the film, for Deerfield is an expatriate. He has not only moved away from the

United States, but he has also seen his memories of the past blurred. In a discussion with his brother at Orly Airport, Deerfield cannot recall the past family events which his brother mentions. He is as figuratively out of focus with his past as the opening dream sequence in the film is literally out of focus.

Clarity starts to come into Deerfield's life through his relationship with Lillian. In metaphorically giving birth to Deerfield through her death, she has awakened his sensitivities to his past—to his roots. Structurally, Pollack visually augments this idea as he presents a picture taken of Deerfield and Lillian at the end of the film. While the dream in the opening is seen as the mind's unfocused recognition of an immediate past, the picture at the end is sharply focused. Because of Lillian's death, Deerfield remains alone at the end as he was in the beginning. In a way, Deerfield has come back to his starting point. He remains alone, but he has gained clarity in his perceptions. With the implication that he returns to America, the circularity of his character is further emphasized; it is as if he is returning to his starting point.

This same idea is more distinctly related in Pollack's film of World War II, *Castle Keep*. With the opening and closing framed in the words "Once upon a time," the film makes us aware of the dreamlike quality and another form of circularity lacking a beginning and end. Rather than the opening nightmare of *Bobby Deerfield*, all of *Castle Keep* is a nightmare in its exposition of war.

The circular structure is of critical thematic importance. Set in a nightmarish world of chaos and slaughter, *Castle Keep* focuses our attention on the timelessness of war. Elements of the dialogue refer to wars long past, and there is no discernible difference between what was then and what is now. As a result of the film's structure, our concern is not with a specific castle or a specific group of men, but with war itself. It is ironic that the words "Once upon a time" should begin and end the film, for they imply the beginning of a fairy tale; all of the elements are present: the castle, the lovely lady of the castle, and the knight on the white horse. The horror is that the fairy tale is a nightmare; that the ongoing pursuit of dreams is grounded in conflict which has neither a beginning nor an end.

Pollack's manipulations of time in *Castle Keep* all directly support the film's dreamlike state: Therese's (Astrid Heeren) jumping her horse over a wall is filmed in slow motion in defiance of the natural progression of time. Major Falconer is stopped in time through Pollack's use of a freeze frame. In the midst of Falconer's shooting at the enemy, we see flashbacks of his affair with Therese. The most prominent restructuring of time, though, is seen at the end of the film, for while we watch the castle burn, we also watch a series of flashbacks which take us all the way back to the beginning of the film.

Time does not progress logically in *Castle Keep,* but it is, after all, a dream in which time is irrelevant. The implements of war may change, but individuals remain essentially the same as they enter into renewed conflicts, having learned nothing from the past.

The same lack of knowledge gained from past experiences also holds true for the character of Katie Morowsky in *The Way We Were.* The very title of the film points to the characters' recollection of the past, but the structure which Pollack gives to the script emphasizes the circularity of the characters' lives. In the development of the relationship between Katie and Hubbell Gardiner, we begin in the middle, then trace the couple's movement up to the present before advancing into the future. Neither individual has changed substantially, yet recollections of their past differences are not enough to keep them from resuming a relationship which is destined to failure. More than any others of Pollack's characters, Katie and Hubbell represent the circularity of life; we twice see them build a relationship which ends in separation.

Pollack's starting in the middle of Katie and Hubbell's story—the original script began at the radio studio—places the first part of the film in flashback. Returning to their initial acquaintance and then moving up to their separation, we see all the factors which point to the improbability of a close relationship between Hubbell as America the Beautiful and Katie as America the Plain. Katie leads a Communist League rally; Hubbell listens. Hubbell races; Katie watches. Katie works as a waitress; Hubbell is the customer. Hubbell's paper is read by the professor; Katie tears hers up in disgust. In spite of their many differences, and in spite of the flashback which makes us feel that Katie is looking back very carefully at her past, Katie takes the drunken Hubbell home in order to rekindle their relationship after the period of separation. She may have seen the way they were, but she has failed to see the way they are.

In starting over, Katie and Hubbell once again go through the motions of togetherness before they separate as they had previously. It is as if they have once again retraced the circle of their lives. Their forward movement has twice brought them back to their starting point, and at the end Pollack again pictures them as they were. Katie maintains her position as the political activist, and her hair is as curly as it was previously. Hubbell remains the image of America the Beautiful, with a suitably beautiful woman by his side. The inevitability of Katie and Hubbell's separation seems clear from our initial observations of their divergent interests, yet the repetition of the cycle intensifies our understanding that individuals remain essentially the same throughout their lives.

Pollack similarly offers a double circle in the relationship between Owen Legate and Alva Starr in *This Property Is Condemned*, but since the film is told in the flashback narration of Willie Starr, it is as much the story of her inability to effect any fundamental change in her life as it is the story of her sister. The futility of life during the Depression is emphasized through the structure of the film, for Willie, dressed in the tattered remains of Alva's clothes, is the obvious parallel to the older sister whose life has amounted to nothing.

The lack of any movement, of any purpose, in the lives of the characters in *This Property Is Condemned* is seen in the juxtaposition of the characters and the Starr Boarding House with the railroad. While trains move rapidly down the tracks next to the Starr house, the people within maintain their static existence. They are apart from any stream of forward progress. Alva may board a train heading for New Orleans and Owen and so move forward and away from her past, but Pollack tells us visually of the impossibility of her making any forward progress. As her train goes over a bridge, it is filmed from a helicopter in a large circular arc. The train may still be moving forward, but it is going nowhere at the same time as the camera alters its forward movement on the screen. Alva's most intimate association with trains is provided by the old railroad car which her father decorated for her. Rusting, dusty, and deteriorated through the passage of time, the car remains a refuge for Alva as an adult as it had for her as a child. The events of her life have not been enough to move her away from what she was as a child. The abandoned railroad car and the Starr Boarding House are adjacent to the main line of the track, but like the characters in the film, they are stationary rather than moving.

Willie is more graphically the same in both the beginning and the end of the film. We see her dressed in Alva's clothes as she begins her story, and we return to her at the end as she completes her narration of the lives of her mother, her sister, and herself. Structuring the film almost completely in flashback brings with it the "Once upon a time" feeling of *Castle Keep*, but Willie's story is more real. She narrates the stories of lives which have gone nowhere, but she herself reflects them as well. Willie begins where Alva left off, but lacking her sister's beauty, sexuality, and once-active environment, Willie's situation is almost hopeless. She stands on the tracks as an awkward adolescent in an ill-fitting dress. Even though she walks on the rails from the siding to the main line, she will in effect make no actual progress as she continues to hide in the dilapidated and condemned structure which was once her home. We watch Willie's movement from an ascending helicopter which begins the circular movement of Alva's train ride to New Orleans although it is frozen before the circle is completed.

The "Once upon a time" quality of Willie's story has a direct bearing to the relationship between Alva and Owen, and since Willie is telling the story, we will never know if it is fact or a young girl's fantasy about her older sister and a handsome visitor to town. Their dreams are in a way like the fairyland picture of Hollywood for Katie and Hubbell in *The Way We Were.* Both couples trace their relationships twice.

The predictability of the dissolution of the relationship between Katie and Hubbell is the same for Alva and Owen in *This Property Is Condemned.* The indication of their two separations is as much visual as it is oral. During a time which Alva and Owen spend together in Dodson, they are never completely alone. Alva is unable to rid herself of her past as former boyfriends intrude, younger boys in town taunt Willie about her sister's reputation, and her mother continually serves as a wedge to force their separation. Their breakup is inevitable since Mrs. Starr does everything within her power to force Alva to provide for her family before she provides for herself.

The same situation reoccurs in New Orleans with the couple's reunion. Although Alva and Owen are physically removed from all whom they knew in Dodson, Alva still cannot escape her past. Ironically, her concern for Willie brings destruction in the form of her mother, who has traced her to New Orleans. Alva is destroyed by her mother's telling Owen the truth of her previous actions, but the Alva who is destroyed at the end is much the same as she was in the beginning. She is charming, personable, and caring, but she is also deceitful. Even her new relationship of apparent trust and concern for Owen is not strong enough for her to admit to the more horrid truths of her past.

As Alva has remained fundamentally unchanged, so Owen has as well. He came into Dodson by himself as a hatchetman for the railroad, and he will continue on to the next town by himself to continue his duties. But while Owen has returned once again to his own starting point, Alva dies. Willie will take over where Alva left off, but her movement seems more a downward spiral than a circle as she begins with only the most minimal of opportunities.

The apparent hopelessness of the lives of the characters in *This Property Is Condemned* is recreated in Pollack's other film of the Depression, *They Shoot Horses, Don't They?* The atrocities which find no conclusion in *This Property Is Condemned* are the agonies which are unending in *They Shoot Horses, Don't They?*

The film is in a category by itself in terms of its structuring of time. Pollack chooses to restrict our view of the dance marathon by holding us within the walls of the Pacific Ballroom throughout all but a very few minutes of the film. We realize that hours and days have elapsed, but time weighs heavily upon both the contestants and us as we move in an agonizingly slow step to the music. None of Pollack's other films has forced us to give such strict attention to the movement of time, and in no other of his films have we been given visual reinforcements of the number of hours which have passed.

The majority of the film moves in a logical time sequence with action which happens realistically, but Pollack uses slow motion and flashbacks in the film as well. While the slow motion used in the dreamlike *Castle Keep* is appropriate and in keeping with the overall feeling of that film, it is in some instances more troublesome in *They Shoot Horses, Don't They?* Flashforwards also may be relevant in other directors' films, but Pollack has not used this device in his other films, and they too are troublesome in *They Shoot Horses.*

The flashforwards and the slow motion shot in the beginning of the film drew Pollack's own criticism in a 1970 article in the *New York Times.* The reporter notes that Pollack " . . . winces at 'the way the flashforwards turned out.'" Pollack also comments that "that stallion running in slow motion looked like a Zee toilet paper commercial."[1]

The problem with these two manipulations of time has everything to do with the attention which Pollack has given in the majority of the film to the excruciatingly slow movement of time for the contestants. Quick flashforwards seem out of place in an environment which is incapable of rapid movement without resultant exhaustion and destruction. They are a confusing device in any film because they leap a span of time which needs to be clarified for us before we can understand the forward image. In *They Shoot Horses,* they fail because their rapidity contradicts the central movement of the film.

Since the slow-motion sequence of the horse is in the beginning of the film, it does not stand out as much. The stallion is a part of Robert's past—part of a past which cannot be recaptured—and so is without the restrictions imposed by the present. The movement back and forth between Robert's presence on the beach and his recollections of the past experiences of his grandfather's shooting of the horse could be equated to Turner's *(Three Days of the Condor)* effort to recall the scene of his friend's murder. The difference, and perhaps the source of the problem, is found in the motivation for the reconstruction of the scene. We understand Turner's effort to recapture the moment, but we do not understand Robert's. Nothing on the beach seems to trigger the memory. The time shifts in the film are not clarified for us until the end when Robert, asked to explain his shooting Gloria, says, "They shoot horses, don't they?"

The connection between Robert's comment and the beginning sequence of the film not only draws the story together, but also underlines the circularity of its structure. Robert has seen and experienced the treatment of people like animals, so his response to Gloria's request shows no fundamental alteration in his response to animals who are suffering. Time has brought a change in the nature of people, but it has not brought about a change in the objective action which they must take. Pollack again uses slow motion when he shows Gloria's death, but in this instance the manipulation of time is more acceptable since it emphasizes the parallel between the stallion and Gloria. The movement is slowed not to emphasize any poetic movement or exploitation of horror. It is as if we are looking at the two situations as Robert is looking at them. It is as if he is apart from both as he acts at the end of the film as his grandfather taught him to act in the beginning.

Although Gloria dies at the end, her outlook on life has undergone no fundamental change from our first view of her. Always tough and always disdainful of life—as seen most poignantly in her response to Ruby's (Bonnie Bedelia) pregnancy—Gloria has repeatedly affirmed the value of death as an escape from the life which she has been enduring. Before meeting Robert, she merely lacked the means to her death.

Such a fusion of the end and the beginning of life is also seen in the elimination derbies of the dance marathon. The visual metaphor here is painfully apparent as the exhausted contestants race around in a furious attempt to survive rather than to win, to be allowed to continue their further agonies. The line painted on the floor is clearly both the start and the finish, yet it marks only the finish for some. Contestants forcibly drag each other about in an effort to win, and the "ancient mariner" (Red Buttons) dies in the process although even he moves across the finish line as Gloria painfully drags his body around the circle.

Pollack uses slow motion in filming the derbies, and his use of it traps us as the contestants have been trapped. We can no longer look at the people as a mass of humanity charging around the circle; instead, we are forced to look at the agony of individuals. Although the derbies last only ten minutes, they seem to go on forever. Pollack gives us no break from our view of tortured humanity, and the dreamlike quality of slow motion equates the derbies to the nightmares of *Castle Keep* and the opening sequence of *Bobby Deerfield*. While Pollack must necessarily compress time in *Horses*, he does not compress it in the derbies; he draws it out through his use of slow motion. We are forced to experience the entire horror of the elimination race, and time weighs as heavily on us as it does on the contestants.

The contestants live in a world without an end, and Pollack further illustrates the point at the conclusion of the film. Gloria is dead and Robert is being taken off to jail, yet the marathon goes on as Rocky announces the elapsed time and the number of couples remaining. While Horace McCoy's novel closes with the end of the marathon, Pollack chooses, characteristically, to leave it open-ended.

The circular structure of all of Pollack's films is consistent with a philosophy that individuals do not undergo significant change in their lives: they do not leap; instead, they take one step. Jeremiah Johnson continues his solitary ways in the end as he did in the beginning, the dance marathon contestants run circular races in their derbies, and Bobby Deerfield races his car past the start-finish line. All return to their starting point. Significantly, though, all strive to continue rather than to give up in defeat. Alan Newell *(Slender Thread)* will return to the Crisis Center, Joe Turner *(Three Days of the Condor)* will remain in America, and Joe Bass *(Scalphunters)* will continue his quest for his stolen furs once again. The circularity of Pollack's vision is not the image of life going nowhere; it is the recognition of humanity's incessant drive to move forward in spite of the forces without and within which bring all individuals back to their starting points.

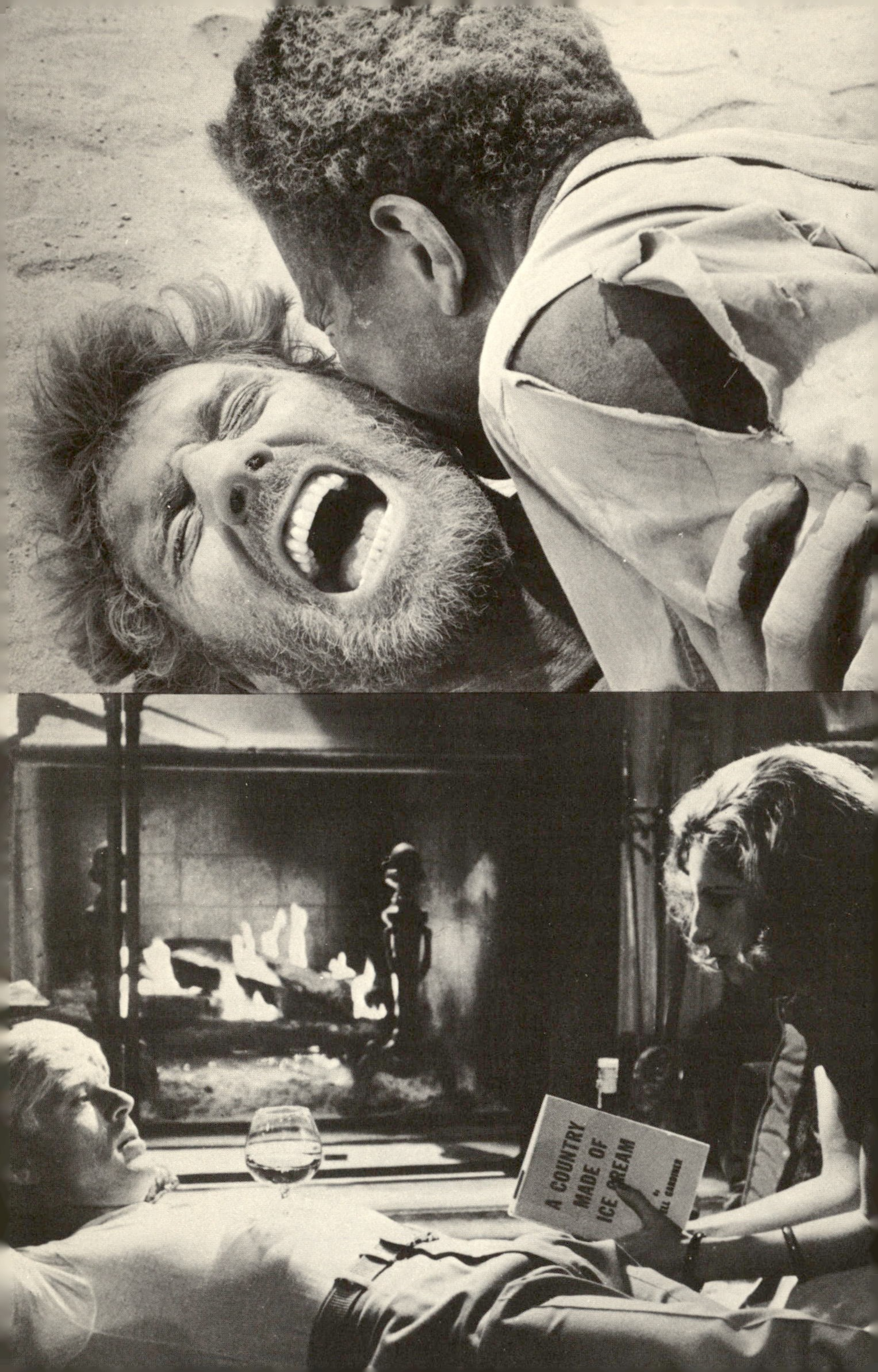
A COUNTRY
MADE OF
ICE

4

In Search of an American Tradition

"I hold all roots in reverence. I think roots are the key to everything. "Bobby Deerfield" deals right on the nose with roots. "Deerfield" is a picture about a rooted community—Italy, thousand year-old culture, and Bobby Deerfield is a man with absolutely no roots at all" —Sydney Pollack

* *

Typically, the films which Sydney Pollack has directed find no common denominator in either genre or setting. Yet, whether the film is set in present-day Japan, nineteenth-century America, or war-torn Belgium during World War II, all of Pollack's films are unified through his interest in the development of America as it seeks a tradition of its own. The family unit in each of Pollack's films serves as the metaphor for America, but the deaths of family members combined with the instability of the family unit itself project a bleak outlook for the future of America. American tradition is a fighting tradition. A Pollack hero may fight to his death for the right to dissent, yet individuals in the American family unit are necessarily isolated. Pollack's heros and heroines reflect a country of isolated individuals of varying backgrounds who identify themselves first by the country of their ancestral origin. They are splintered remnants of former traditions who have come together as a sum of the parts which is called America.

Pollack's films do express the growth of America. Until the 1975 production of *The Yakuza*, Pollack had concentrated his efforts on films depicting America's past. *The Scalphunters* and *Jeremiah Johnson* illustrate a migrant people in its chaotic attempt to dominate the native Indians and so impose its own identity on the fledgling nation. *This Property Is Condemned* and *They Shoot Horses, Don't They?* evoke the Depression years and individuals who lack a positive identity as

Photos: (top) Joseph Lee (Ossie Davis) gains the upper hand over Joe Bass (Burt Lancaster) in The Scalphunters; *(bottom) Katie (Barbra Streisand) discusses Hubbel's (Robert Redford) book in* The Way We Were. *(courtesy of Sydney Pollack)*

much as the country does. *Castle Keep,* a reflection of the American fighting spirit of World War II, similarly exhibits a people who trace circles in their search for an identity. *The Slender Thread,* a film set in the early 1950s, presents an even more clearly defined image of an isolated American who teeters on the brink of insanity as she searches for her identity. The isolation of this individual—and the instability of her family, founded in deceit—directly parallels the development of the American family as a whole.

Pollack's films which present modern American society are films of greater optimism about the potential cohesiveness of a nation. They express the necessity of forward movement which the previous films show, but they also portray individuals who come to terms with themselves. They express a spirit of independence which results from a recognition of the importance of a unified family and national spirit.

The Way We Were is an affirmation of a tradition inexorably bound to honor the freedom of dissent. *Three Days of the Condor* expresses the importance of the individual's fundamental right to expose deceit in government. The representation of the American tradition in the Far East and in Europe is seen in *The Yakuza* and in *Bobby Deerfield,* for in these two films the American heritage is sharply contrasted with cultures and traditions much older than its own.

The Developing Nation

The early history of America as represented in *The Scalphunters* and *Jeremiah Johnson* is a statement of the instability of the country as it is reflected through fragmented families. Unity exists neither in the country as a whole nor in the warring factors which seek to preserve their traditions.

Jeremiah Johnson is an early representation of the spirit of dissent which Pollack later repeats as a fundamental part of the American tradition. Jeremiah must take refuge in the wild since he is a deserter from military service to his country. He must isolate himself from the remainder of the new civilization if he is to be able to express his personal views.

As Jeremiah learns to live in the uncivilized mountains, so he must learn the ways of the "uncivilized" Indians. He must learn their history, and he must learn their traditions if he is to be at peace with them. Jeremiah learns while other white men fail. The failure and disintegration of one pioneering white family is a catalyst to the creation of his own family as Jeremiah takes a muted "son" who has been devastated by the atrocities of the Indians who have responded to the supposed civilization which encroaches on their territory. Jeremiah then takes an Indian wife, and his family metaphorically speaks of the composite of the American nation in the mid-1800s.

The savage annihilation of Jeremiah's family is the resurgence of the native Indians protecting their traditions. Their retaliation for Jeremiah's intrusion into their sacred burial ground is both vicious and pure. A new civilization which respects neither the customs of another nor the importance of the representation of the dead spirit of another's civilization should not endure. Jeremiah survives because he has understood the ways of the Indians. He has discarded the literal and figurative clothing of his "civilization" in his donning of the trappings of the wilderness and its people. He will merely coexist with the Indians, though. He will never become one with them, just as America will remain merely the sum total of its disparate parts. While the Indians fight to hold on to their long-established traditions, fighting itself is the tradition for the emerging America which seeks personal gain as its goal.

Jeremiah Johnson's identification with the Indian culture is similar to the Joseph Lee character in *The Scalphunters*. Like Jeremiah, Joseph Lee is out of step with an ill-defined civilization which has allowed a slave the means but not the purpose for his classical education. He, like the exaggerated, extreme representative of civilized man completely out of tune with the rudimentary mores of a developing nation, seeks refuge in the wilderness like Jeremiah.

The master/slave relationship between Joseph Lee and the illiterate Joe Bass is an ironic metonym for the absurdity of a new civilization in chaos. Eastern civilization is out of tune in the West.

Pollack effectively illustrates the disparity by providing the marauding scalphunters with a covered wagon containing a brass bed. The conflict of civilizations continues in the alliance between Jim Howie and Kate (Shelley Winters). She will live with a man who kills Indians for a living, but she will not tolerate his chewing tobacco or hanging the smelly scalps on their wagon. Their tentative union as a rudimentary family is an expression of the unstable condition of the nation. Swift and probable death is a way of life. Jim Howie slaughters Indians—after they have become drunk on the civilizer's alcohol—in order to claim the bounty promised by the new civilization of mankind which hopes to "exterminate the brutes."

Significantly, Joseph Lee, the adopted member of the Indian tribe, kills Jim Howie when his deceitful game of death fails. Death to the conquerers of the Indian tradition is matter-of-fact. It has no ceremony. The scalped Indians are left to rot in the rivers and on the sun-parched desert. Their own dead find either a similar fate, or they are provided with a wooden cross which is but a tentative symbol of a civilization which may prove to be tentative itself.

Pollack's definitive statement about the tentative quality of the American family comes at the death of Jim Howie. Kate momentarily contemplates her own fate, then looks at the victorious Kiowas and says, "What the hell, they're only men." One "family" is as good as another; her own obscure heritage is of little importance.

The pioneers of the American tradition seen in these two films show little respect for the life and the more established traditions of the Indians. Their quest, like the quest of Americans in Pollack's later films, is for tangible gain. Only the isolated individuals of the new civilization, Griz and Jeremiah in *Jeremiah Johnson*, and Joe Bass and Joseph Lee in *The Scalphunters*, who have cast off their dubious heritage are cognizant of the intrinsic values of the Indian culture. They are also the individuals who have been denied stable families. As in Pollack's other films, they are metonyms for the developing nation as a whole.

The Depression Years

The Depression years in America are a mighty leap from the early founding of the country, but little has changed in substance. While tangible gain was the goal for the advancing civilization of pioneers in the 1800s, it remains the goal of the people living during the Depression. The spirit of the country, its heritage and tradition, is defined by money and the power which goes with it. This condition becomes paradoxical and exaggerated during the Depression because of the inaccessibility of the coveted goals. The family unit which Pollack presents has either disintegrated completely in the spiritual sense, or it has been again destroyed by death as the final blow to any apparent unity. Prosperity has died, and its death has claimed the American spirit as well. Individuals are characterized by a savage quest for money to such an extent that they think only of themselves. Even members of their immediate families become secondary to their interest in money. When one woman's husband falls to the floor from exhaustion during one of the derbies, she hits him and screams for him to get up instead of showing any sensitivity to his condition. When another man drags his pregnant wife around during the derbies, he shows concern for her but then pulls her around the circle anyhow. Such is the metaphor of the splintered American family which continues to have no organic unity.

The Starr family of *This Property Is Condemned* is Sydney Pollack's primary example of the continued instability of the family unit. Alva Starr, her sister, Willie, and their mother, Hazel, are remnants of a fatherless family. Any unity among them can be found only in their efforts to secure a wealthy provider for Alva. Tradition is unimportant. Hazel seeks to align her daughter with an older man whose wife has been seriously ill for years. Stability is to be achieved through money rather than through marriage. Like the slaughter of the Indians in *The Scalphunters*, personal gain is the motivating force.

Alva's sudden marriage to her mother's lover, J.J. Nichols, (Charles Bronson) and her subsequent hasty flight to Owen Legate further point out the instability of the family unit and the ill-defined traditions of a chaotic nation. Alva's failure to tell Owen that she has married merely compounds her singular quest for self. Her values have nothing to do with her family; she is concerned only with herself.

When Alva experiences some happiness with Owen, even this small family unit must crumble. Her self-seeking mother is the means to its destruction and to Alva's death. Owen and Willie remain, but Willie is the victim. Isolated through the death of her sister and the desertion of her mother, Willie wears the fragments of Alva's dress, clutches a doll which is a compilation of two, and says of the Starr family boarding house and of herself, "This property is condemned, but there ain't nothing wrong with it." She is condemned by a nation without a unifying tradition, a nation which contains merely coexisting individuals who are unable to come together into a solidified whole. Willie's isolation is like that of Jeremiah Johnson, but it has been intensified because the noble savages have been eliminated. Willie has no escape to another culture. Her isolation among the crowded isolations of others is a product of her heritage.

The same sense of isolation is more graphically shown in *They Shoot Horses, Don't They?*, and the goal of the dance marathon is Hazel's goal in *This Property Is Condemned*—money. Money can buy happiness; it is the American way. Crowds cheer as they watch the animalistic competitors cling savagely to each other in their effort to remain standing until they are the last couple to stand. The crowd throws coins in a special tribute to a job well done. Every ounce of energy is directed to monetary gain.

The family units presented in the dance marathon are bestial. Nothing is sacred. Even motherhood is debased as the pregnant woman is dragged about the dance floor by her husband. The most tragic figure, Gloria, is the epitome of the futility of the American way. She speaks in fragments of her splintered family. She is broken, completely isolated, and entrapped in a culture without direction or purpose. Her decision to commit suicide is horrid but plausible. Robert's decision to help her end her life is overwhelming.

Pollack is presenting an agonizing exposé of the state to which America has come. Denied the attainment of a materialistic core, the center cannot hold. Gloria becomes nothing more than a trapped animal. She has lost her spirit, and she sees the futility of the race toward an empty goal.

Death also takes the "ancient mariner" during one of the derbies, but Gloria drags his lifeless body along so that she won't be eliminated. Crowds cheer; celebrities are introduced; death is incidental in a nation gone mad.

The same matter-of-factness of the sailor's death cannot be applied to Gloria. Hers is too specific an event in that she moves outside of the applauded insanity. Being such, the response to Robert's part in it must come through specific laws which isolate insanity rather than applaud it.

World War II and Its Aftermath

The isolation and lack of purpose of Gloria's life finds a direct parallel in Pollack's film of World War II, *Castle Keep*. The isolation of individuals is even more severe in this film than it was in *They Shoot Horses, Don't They?*, for the scene has shifted to Europe. The family unit has become a unit of soldiers. Americans with their tradition of fighting are given the task of preserving a segment of European culture. The task itself is a contradiction to their way of life and to the fighting spirit which is so typically American.

Settled in a magnificent castle which they choose to defend, the Americans led by Major Falconer fight for an ideal which is not within their compass of understanding. Ironically, they are unable to appreciate the tangible manifestations of the culture which they are trying to save. In effect, they are still fighting the Indians; their interest is in the battle itself, fighting for the sake of fighting, the American spirit. That which is destroyed in the process is of less consequence than the battle itself.

The Americans are out of place in the castle's aesthetic environment. They draw beards and moustaches on statues; they use wine bottles for bowling pins; they destroy statues, which bleed when hit; they kill the music which emanates from the forest; they drive tanks through sculptured evergreens; they transform art into flesh.

Their failure to recognize the aesthetic value of art is also apparent in their misguided sense of morality and love. Sergeant Rossi seeks comfort with the baker's wife. Falconer covets Therese, the wife of the castle's owner, and the troops find companionship with the local brothel women. Perhaps the most clearly defined statement of the nature of the American quest for love is seen in Corporal Clearboy's love for the perfection of the Volkswagen. Driving it out of the castle moat after having been deceived into jumping out of the window of the keep, Clearboy traces circles in the snow with the car. He is constantly moving, but he has nowhere to go. His mechanical ideal is both tangible and functional, but he can only guide it in circular patterns which must necessarily return to their starting points.

The family units of *Castle Keep* are as nondirectional as Clearboy's Volkswagen. They are temporary. They move, but they too are headed nowhere. Like the Volkswagen, the women lovers and companions of the soldiers are left behind when the troops leave in either victory or death. Characteristically, death destroys the family units. Those of *Castle Keep* are as unstable in their origins as the family units seen in *Jeremiah Johnson, The Scalphunters,* and *They Shoot Horses, Don't They?*

The black author among the soldiers who lives to tell their story conveys the history of his warring family. They held tenaciously to a tradition of fighting in an aesthetic environment which surpasses the naturally aesthetic surroundings of the wilds of *Jeremiah Johnson.* Their enemy encircles them, but their isolation is not simply geographical; it is cultural as well. Their insensitivity to the aesthetic values of a civilization from which they have been transplanted by time and distance further extends the disparity between their American tradition and the European culture. Their movement is clearly defined, but they continue to return to their starting point in the wilderness of America's origin.

Perhaps Pollack's most precise statement of the nature of America can be found in the title of Hubbell Gardiner's book in *The Way We Were: A Country Made of Ice Cream*. Ever-changing, the country is without a base.

The Way We Were encompasses the late 1930s, the 1940s, and the 1950s, and it projects the splintered extremes found in the American nation as characterized by one American family: Hubbell Gardiner, the "all-American" intelligent athlete; his wife, Katie Morowsky, the plain Jewish activist who takes a definitive stand, and their unseen daughter, the product of a union which was more figmentary than real.

The extremes of the family are the extremes of a nation which seeks some unified whole. Katie distributes leaflets at college for the Young Communist League, but later the McCarthy investigation of Hollywood personalities bans anyone who is even remotely suspected of an affiliation with communism. Hubbell is the representative of a new sort of aristocracy in the American search for a definable culture. He may be one of the cultured, yet he willingly sacrifices principles in order to maintain his position at the top of the pay scale. The aesthetic concern of his brand of culture and aristocracy is personal beauty, the aesthetic which the Old World cultures perceive has become in America the perceiver himself.

Pollack visually explains Hubbell's presence as the image of the American aesthetic in a scene depicting a private screening in Hollywood. A Picasso painting is accidentally ripped by a hidden microphone, and then Hubbell moves between the projector and the screen and so becomes part of the aesthetic.

The Gardiner family communicates, but thick glass separates Katie and Hubbell as she flicks switches in the control room. They see, but they do not touch. They are isolated in their union as Gloria and Robert in *Horses*, Major Falconer and Therese in *Castle Keep*, Owen Legate and Alva Starr in *This Property Is Condemned*, and democracy and communism.

Like Pollack's other films, death brings about the destruction of the family unit. For the Gardiner family, the death is Hubbell's spiritual death in his acquiescence in accepting the mandate of the McCarthy commission. Hubbell later remarries, but to one of "his own." Katie also remarries, but she too marries one who implicitly accepts her as she is. The union of Katie and Hubbell could not survive any more than could a union of any other such extremes in America. Like the presence of Indians, Puerto Ricans, Germans, and other cultures in America today and in the past, such widely separate cultures can merely coexist as they form Italian-American clubs and set aside holidays to remember saints of their ancestor's countries. They are pigeonholed by their name and not by their birth. Katie and Hubbell are Pollack's metaphor for the composition of America. It is amorphous, a "country made of ice cream." Its substance is defined by the decade rather than by the century.

The decade of the 1950s, in which the Gardiners separate, is also the setting for another of Pollack's unstable families which serves as a metaphor for the American family. The Dyson family of Pollack's first film, *The Slender Thread*, is a complex study of a family's inability to communicate. The family is reflective of an American heritage founded in deceit, perpetrated by illusion, and saved by a new generation of the educated.

But the family is struck by the spiritual death of Inga Dyson. She, like Hubbell Gardiner, sidesteps the truth in order to maintain an illusion of righteousness. Neither of them is far removed from the civilizers of America who slaughtered the Kiowa Indians for a monetary reward.

Inga's marriage to Mark Dyson while pregnant with another man's child is a chaotic beginning to any hope for family unity, but that Steven is for years led to believe that Chris is his own son is almost unbelievable. Such an act is a manifestation of a heritage which seeks security at any cost. It represents a civilization which expresses a greater interest in the tangible comforts than it does in the principle of the matter. In a way, Inga is like Alva Starr seeking Owen Legate when she has just recently married J. J..

Inga's spirit is dead almost before it has had a chance for life. Her illegitimate pregnancy isolates her from others in the society, but her inability to confront the truth brings yet greater isolation for her. Like Gloria's plight in *They Shoot Horses*, the soldier's plight in *Castle Keep*, and Jeremiah's plight in *Jeremiah Johnson*, no escape is possible without isolation or death as the result.

Inga's rescue by the young, inexperienced Alan Newell at the Crisis Center is a rescue of the most tentative sort. He has saved her life, but for what purpose? The situation has not altered. Inga will go back to her home, but the deceit which she carried into her marriage can never be erased. Mark can try to understand her motivation, but he can never fully understand his being deceived for so many years. Inga obscured the truth from herself as America continues to obscure the truth of its founding from itself. The reward for such self-deception is materialistic, financial security, and it is as savage as scalping Indians for profit or taking their land for personal use.

Into the Seventies: At Home and Abroad

The same sort of financial self interest is also the interest in *Three Days of the Condor*, and the telephone is as critical to Joe Turner in saving his life and the spirit of the American people as it was to Inga Dyson. The difference between the 1950s and the 1970s is the difference in technological sophistication. Using telephones, computers, and tape recorders, Joe Turner experiences all levels of mechanical communication. As a brilliant practitioner of the art, he at times serves as an intermediary as the machines talk to themselves. With such an intensity of mechanical communication, the individual takes on a role of lesser importance than the machines themselves. Individual isolation in the 1970s is even more pronounced than it was in the 1950s of *The Slender Thread*.

Like the instability of the Dyson family in *The Slender Thread*, such instability is exaggerated in *Three Days of the Condor*. In fact, complete families do not appear in the film. Joe Turner may seek aid from a married couple who are his friends, but the husband is absent; he is killed trying to help Joe. Individuals remain isolated, and the sound of computers printing out data punctuates the film while underlying the dominance of the machine.

All possible alliances with women for Joe Turner are effectively destroyed throughout the film. The relationship which he has with Janice (Tina Chen) at the office is ended when she is killed. Joe later sleeps with Kathy Hale, but their union is the momentary comfort sought by two lonely and desperate people rather than a romantic union. As his hostage and his means of escape, Kathy is an object for Joe. She uses him as well in her escape from a rather routine existence. Her black-and-white photographs reflect the two of them with their isolated subjects placed in cold environments.

Joe attempts to uncover deceit, but he must travel roads of assassination and intrigue. He can trust no one; he can tell no one of his discoveries. His discovered truths about covert operations in a governmental intelligence agency would be believed by few. Those who do believe him at headquarters must kill him since they are the ones seeking world manipulation for their own financial gain. America has gone completely insane; money and world-wide power are synonymous with tradition.

Like the Watergate story, Joe's story is told to the *New York Times*. Unlike Watergate and much like Sydney Pollack's films, the hero does not rise triumphantly. He must remain isolated to an even greater extent than he was previously. In his pursuit of a just American society, and in his success in seeing justice move into operation, Joe Turner must remain hidden from the materialists whose lives he has destroyed. We can have hope that justice will prevail in America, but we have little hope that Joe Turner will ever be able to move out of his isolation.

Such isolation is also the material of *The Yakuza*, but the film's treatment of an American in a Japanese culture graphically illustrates one American's attempt to surpass his obscure heritage so that he can communicate within the context of an older civilization. Significantly, *The Yakuza* is a film about the disintegration of Japanese traditions, the disintegration of the principles behind one's duty and obligation to family. The catalyst to the disintegration is Western—it is American.

The main character, Harry Kilmer, is an isolated American who has no American family. In the spirit of family unity which Pollack presented with the soldiers of *Castle Keep*, Kilmer agrees to journey to Japan in order to help rescue the kidnapped daughter of a friend. We learn that the yakuza have kidnapped the daughter because her father has taken money from the yakuza without giving them the guns which were part of the deal.

The Yakuza presents substantive examples of the Americanization of Japan. All of it is commercial. Neon lights spell in English the names of American products while Japanese characters glow beside them; the young wear blue denim; kitchens contain Brillo soap pads; and nightclubs mix the sounds of Oriental minor keys with a song of America's heritage, "My Darlin' Clementine." Even Harry's gift to Eiko, his lover during the American occupation of Japan, is distinctly American—a bar, which will bring her financial profit.

Harry has a family of sorts with Eiko and her daughter, but it is as tentative as the one which Inga Dyson had. Like Inga, Eiko has deceived Harry in her failure to tell him that Tanaka Ken is her husband rather than her brother.

Tanaka Ken is labeled as a "relic of a former age" when he despairs over the immensity of the act which he must perform in killing his nephew, but when the American Kilmer seeks to share in the responsibility and closeness of the tragedy, he is reminded that he is not a member of the family.

Tanaka Ken's amputation of a finger and offering of it to his brother after killing his son is within the tradition of honor and respect to family members. It represents his recognition of the sorrow which he has brought to his brother; it represents his recognition of the dishonor which he has brought to his family.

Kilmer, a relic from the past like Tanaka Ken, surpasses his American heritage when he too severs his finger and presents it to Tanaka Ken for bringing dishonor to him through his love affair with Eiko and for being responsible for their daughter's death. Yet Kilmer does not become a part of the family; he remains an American.

When Kilmer's plane climbs into the sky on its return to America, it heads directly into a massive black cloud. Kilmer is to return to his homeland, but it is a home without a family unit, and it is a homeland which is incapable of understanding an Old World tradition which demands a symbolic atonement for bringing disgrace into the family.

In an even more definitive view of the nature of the American way, *Bobby Deerfield* sets an American in the midst of a European culture. Deerfield's isolation is self-imposed, and rather than seeking the closeness of a family relationship, he severs all of his family ties by leaving his homeland. His separation from his family is so intense that he has even forgotten the events of his childhood.

Rather than merely seeking the tangible rewards of the American way of life, Deerfield has become, like Hubbell Gardiner, that sought-after object; he glories in his stature as one of America's products. With his red, white, and blue racing uniform, he is the American influence abroad. His flag may be American, but his other flags at trackside are the Marlboro and Texaco flags.

American products may seem to be his identity, but his real identity is the financial gain associated with his endorsement of products. He can easily transfer his identity to European products as he poses for pictures in front of the Eiffel Tower while endorsing Martini and Rossi vermouth. He will also promote a Seiko watch that becomes so much a part of him that he wears it during his racing and during his lovemaking.

His complete isolation and lack of identity with a family commitment lead him to a mechanical and unemotional existence. As an ironic twist from Pollack's previous films, Deerfield is not the product of an unstable family with an alcoholic mother even though he invents such a story for Lillian. Yet he has denied his family both in thought and deed. He places geographical distance between himself and them by choosing to live in Paris. He may live in a cacophony of ever-present death at the track, but the unemotional state which he has achieved through his denial of personal relationships makes him the winner at the track.

Deerfield will attend the funeral of a fellow racer, but he will show no emotion. He will visit a hospitalized colleague who was paralyzed in a fiery crash, but he goes only to determine the cause of the crash. While the one is physically paralyzed, Deerfield remains emotionally paralyzed. He has reached an emotionally isolated position essential to his victory in racing and to his reaping the financial benefits associated with it.

The emotional exuberance which Lillian offers to Deerfield is the contrast between the European and the American cultures. Lillian will take chances, and those which she takes recognize her vulnerability as a human being.

Deerfield takes chances on the racetrack, but such chances are calculated risks. He has covered every angle. He has made sure that the mechanics are sound. Like Lillian, he travels in the midst of death also, but his vulnerability is merely physical. Both he and Lillian will come to death on their own terms. Essentially, they are one and the same in their attitudes about death and taking chances. The difference lies in their heritage—in the isolation resulting from ill-defined tradition of the American and his family unit, and in the family warmth and well-defined traditions of the Europeans.

Lillian reaches out to Bobby by seeming as emotionally uninvolved with him as he is with her. She will sleep with him, but she will leave him a clue in the morning which indicates that she has gone flying in a balloon with another man. She will take a chance, but it is an uncalculated chance. Through her actions, Lillian teaches Deerfield to take a chance. His is to make himself vulnerable by exposing his past. When he shows her old family pictures, when he does his imitation of Mae West, and when he renders his monotonal version of "Boo hoo, you've got me cryin' for you" he is beginning to recognize his link with his American heritage.

Like the story which Lillian tells about death and birth, Lillian's death brings the emotional birth of Deerfield. In his tentative recognition of the importance of his family, he does not enter the dark cloud of Harry Kilmer in *The Yakuza*, but he travels through a tunnel of intermittent light until he exits into the totally blinding light of the outside. Such intensity of light is as ambiguous as the extremes contained within the American nation. The light is a guarded optimism about an American who sees, but it is about one who sees so much that he is blinded; such blindness is hopefully only temporary. Significantly, Pollack ends the film with an American tourist's picture of Deerfield and Lillian—a snapshot which Deerfield could have obtained only if he has returned to his family home in New Jersey.

Sydney Pollack shows throughout his films a concern for some sort of definition of America. Founded in savage annihilation of Indian natives, forwarded by an obsession with financial gain which sublimates conscience, and composed of widely different kinds of people who divide their identity with their ancestral past and their American present, the America which Pollack presents is one of isolated individuals who can merely coexist without ever reaching any unity. With the fighting spirit as their tradition, they have only that aggression to cling to for their base. The result is a country of individuals who can either move with the masses in their quest for financial success or seek to overthrow such a tradition and by doing so necessarily isolate themselves from the insanity of the financial facts of life.

5

From Aggressive to Passive: The Nature of Men

"*. . . The men differ in all of my films. In a film like "Three Days of the Condor," though, what's enjoyable is watching a small man taking on a huge system and displaying his strength and capacity for growth in that way*" —Sydney Pollack

* *

The male actors whom Sydney Pollack has used for leading roles in his films at once suggest a virile aggressiveness which is implied through their very presence on the screen. Whether Robert Redford, Burt Lancaster, Robert Mitchum, Peter Falk, or Al Pacino, the actor himself defines his apparent role. Under Pollack's direction, though, audience expectations are not always fulfilled because of the complexity of each of the male characters. The range of the character which Pollack explores moves, ironically, from Redford to Redford. On the one end we see the physical aggressiveness of Jeremiah Johnson, but on the other we see the cardboard-cutout passiveness of Hubbell Gardiner in *The Way We Were*. The majority of the male leads are variations of the Jeremiah Johnson character in their assertiveness, their attempts to preserve through destruction, and in their roles as principled individuals who illustrate a sensitive concern for others. At the opposite extreme, Hubbell Gardiner and Bobby Deerfield stand out as passive individuals who pursue their course through life unemotionally. They illustrate a phase of humanity which is not seen in the other major male roles or in the lead roles for women in Pollack's films.

Jeremiah Johnson: The Rise to Purposefulness

The epitome of masculinity defined by aggressive behavior is seen in Jeremiah Johnson. Although Jeremiah is naive when he first enters the mountain wilderness, he soon learns the means to his survival. Iron-

Photo: Robert (Michael Sarrazin) supports Gloria (Jane Fonda) as they endure the horrors of the marathon in They Shoot Horses, Don't They?. *(credit: Museum of Modern Art/Film Stills Archive)*

ically, Jeremiah's very lack of aggressiveness characterized him at the beginning of the film. As a pacifist, he deserted the conflicts of war in favor of the serenity of the wilderness only to learn that his survival was directly linked to his willingness and ability to assert himself. While much of Jeremiah's training comes from Griz in his teaching Jeremiah the means to his survival in hunting, Jeremiah also shows his ability to defend himself from the continued Indian attacks. An attacking Indian may hold the upper hand in his landing on Jeremiah without warning, but Jeremiah manages not only to escape, but to win each time.

Jeremiah's aggressiveness is further seen in his launching his own attack against a group of Indians after they have slaughtered his wife and their "son". He does not calmly wait for them to come to him; he moves against them in a one-against-many situation. His emergence as the victor offers proof of his courage and virility. He becomes a legend in the land because of his skills in battle, and his legendary status justifies his position as a "man's man."

Although such physical ability and courage would be enough to define Jeremiah's character, Pollack characteristically adds a dimension of sensitivity. We are to see Jeremiah's concern for people in our total view of him. Jeremiah is capable of destroying others, yet he is also capable of tenderness.

In general, the sensitivity of the rugged mountain man is seen in his relationship with women and children. The scenes in which we see Jeremiah's attempt to comfort the crazed pioneer woman who has seen part of her family slaughtered by Indians makes Jeremiah less than a legend and more of a human for us. The Jeremiah who destroys is also an individual who shows compassion in his taking the woman's muted son along with him. The scenes which show the strengthening bond between man and boy speak of Jeremiah's inner strength of character. Jeremiah is not a miracle worker; he is unable to make the boy speak, but his failure with the boy lends credence to his character.

Jeremiah's relationship with Swan, his Indian wife, offers further illustrations of the warm and compassionate side of his nature. He not only teaches her his language, but he learns some of her Indian dialect as well. He may find the food which she makes intolerable, but he does not throw it away in disgust. Rather, he finds inconspicuous ways to hide it so that Swan cannot see his displeasure.

Jeremiah's interaction with Swan places her on a level which is

Photos: Two aspects of Jeremiah Johnson, (top) readying himself for the next Indian attack and (bottom) interacting with his wife Swan and the child. *(courtesy of Sydney Pollack)*

roughly equivalent to his. They build the cabin together and then play together. Jeremiah may be the rugged individualist who is capable of withstanding countless Indian attacks, but he is also a warm and compassionate individual who treats others with dignity and respect.

One of the major ironies of the film concerns the dilemma which Jeremiah faces in helping the rescue party get to the stranded white settlers. His is a decision which pits respect for the living against respect for the dead. Although we would think him a callous person if he failed to lead the rescue group to the stranded people, he must display an ostensible contempt for the Indians' sacred burial ground by taking the rescuers through it. His insistence upon silence in the graveyard is his partial atonement to the Indians, but his family is destroyed because he has gone against the very principle of respect which he himself has personified.

Jeremiah Johnson may be a legend to those who only hear tales of his abilities to fend off attacking Indians, but we see a much more detailed image of him. He is first an inexperienced outsider who seems destined to freeze in the mountains before he acquires the necessary survival skills. He struggles, yet he learns. He suffers, yet he moves on. He is admirable for both his physical strength and for his strength of character as well.

Harry Kilmer

These same physical and inner strengths are also seen in the character of Harry Kilmer in *The Yakuza*. He too is characterized by a physical aggressiveness which is but one aspect of his character. He too is faced with a dilemma which has no apparent resolution, and he too is a compassionate individual whose life is guided more by his concern for others than for himself.

Kilmer's obligation to others is the force which, like Jeremiah, brings him into conflict. When George Tanner asks Kilmer to travel to Japan to help him free his daughter from the yakuza, Kilmer does not hesitate. He may not be aware of the magnitude of his decision any more than Jeremiah was aware of the magnitude of his, but he goes because he is acquainted with a member of the yakuza who may be able to help.

Kilmer's acquaintance with Tanaka Ken is also linked to his compassionate character. He met Tanaka Ken through Eiko, and he knew Eiko because he helped her when she was desperately seeking medicine for her daughter. Like Jeremiah's ability to adapt to a different civilization, Kilmer also learns to adapt to the traditions of the Japanese culture. He is sensitive to his position as an outsider, but he adopts many of their customs as his measure of respect for them. The warm reception which Kilmer receives from Eiko and her daughter when he returns to Japan speaks of Kilmer's past relationship with the individuals and their culture.

The other side of Kilmer's character illustrates the physical strength and daring seen in Jeremiah. When fighting becomes the only means which will free Tanner's daughter, Kilmer does not hesitate. With Tanaka Ken, he will go into a room filled with yakuza in an attempt to save the girl. He does not back down in the face of apparently impossible odds; like Jeremiah, he emerges victoriously because of his strength and ability.

The dilemmas which Kilmer faces are found first in his attacking the yakuza and so bringing their revenge upon his own head, and second, and more importantly, in his need to atone to Tanaka Ken for his actions. He had unknowingly created a separation between Eiko and Tanaka Ken, and he was indirectly responsible for the death of their daughter.

In the first situation, Kilmer's choice is not an arduous one. Courageous, and thinking first about the girl to be rescued, he willingly places his own life on the line. The second dilemma offers greater evidence of the total character of Pollack's male leads.

Kilmer has shown courage and compassion in saving both Tanner's and Eiko's daughters. He could not have predicted either that Eiko's daughter would be killed as a result of his relationship with Tanner, or that his aid to Eiko would result in her separation from Tanaka Ken, who was presumed killed in the war when Kilmer lived with her.

Like Jeremiah, Kilmer's obligation is to the living, and his responsibility is to Tanaka Ken in particular. Although Kilmer was not wrong in helping Eiko, he was wrong to take Tanaka Ken's place before knowing that he was dead. If Kilmer had no compassion, he would walk away from the situation knowing that he had at least saved Tanner's daughter. But Kilmer is sensitive to others. The man who walks into a bloody confrontation with the yakuza is also the man who participates in a symbolic act of atonement which illustrates his sensitivity to Japanese tradition. Our initial view of Kilmer is Pollack's visual offering of the complexity of his character. His physical size and bearing attest to his strength, but his concern for flowers and plants attests to his sensitivity.

Joe Turner

Many of the same qualities seen in Jeremiah Johnson and Harry Kilmer are also a part of the Joe Turner character in *Three Days of the Condor*. Turner has the aggressiveness of the others as well as the sensitivity, but his position of strength seems diluted because he is one against hundreds rather than one against several. His physical battles are not against his actual opponents but rather against the instruments of others' wills.

While Jeremiah and Kilmer consciously place themselves in positions which bring about conflict and death, Turner is instead trapped in such a situation. He is never the hunter; he is the hunted. Although his situation is different from the others, Turner yet manifests his physical strength and ability when he is literally under fire. He does all that he can to avoid battle, but when an assassin comes into the apartment disguised as a mailman, Turner uses every means at his disposal to destroy his attacker.

Turner shows the aggressive qualities of Kilmer and Jeremiah, but his is more of an intellectual matter. Rather than relying on physical strength, Turner uses his intelligence to destroy the enemy. We see that he can win a physical battle, but we see also that he is fighting a network of intelligent and cunning men who have been succeeding in their plot to gain a monopoly on oil through intelligent strategy rather than through physical strength.

The dilemma which Turner faces is much like that of Jeremiah and Kilmer in that he places his life in jeopardy when he opposes a group of men. Like Jeremiah and Kilmer he could take no action and so ensure the continuance of his life, but also like them he decides to act on principle. Although adequately warned and although fully knowledgeable of the possible consequences Turner decides to turn over to the *New York Times* his information about the covert actions of the CIA. His interest is with the living and with those to follow him.

This concern for future nameless individuals is not as readily apparent in Turner's daily life. We see little actual warm interaction like that between Kilmer and Eiko. Turner has neither Jeremiah's actual family nor Kilmer's artificial one. Turner lives in an insensitive twentieth-century American world which allows at best only tentative, fleeting concern for others. Pollack gives us instances of Turner's concern for others, but they are as self-centered as they are temporary.

In the beginning of the film, we see the implication of a relationship between Turner and Janice. Through hand and eye contact between them, we sense a tentative relationship. Yet, the American-Chinese relationship is the logical progression of the American-Indian and the American-Japanese units as Janice's death comes abruptly before she and Turner have had the time to become more stable in their relationship. We may sense Turner's concern for her, but the only concern which we see comes after her brutal death as he gently moves the hair out of her eyes.

The same idea holds as well for Turner's friendship with Sam, a friend who was duped into bringing Turner into a vulnerable position in an alleyway. While we see that Sam's wife has set the table for dinner for four which was to include Turner and Janice, Turner's concern when he arrives at the apartment is for the safety of Sam's widow and himself. His situation does not allow him the time to express his concerns in any but a cursory manner.

Turner's relationship with Kathy Hale is also similar. Their intimate relationship may seem to be like that of Jeremiah and Swan, but it is much more tentative. It is New York City compared with the uncivilized West. Turner must force Kathy to help him to uncover the intrigue in the CIA, and their relationship is that of the bleak pictures on Kathy's walls to which Pollack intercuts throughout their lovemaking. Both characters are sensitive to their desperate need for each other, but they yet retain their anonymity in their bleak worlds.

The Joe Turner character is representative of the majority of Pollack's male leads. They maintain a physically aggressive quality which is secondary to their natures, they show a sensitive concern for others which is transient at best, and they face decisions which test their strengths as principled beings.

Major Falconer

The decision of Major Falconer in *Castle Keep* directly parallels those of Jeremiah Johnson, Harry Kilmer, and Joe Turner. Faced with the approaching enemy and the decision either to surrender the castle, full of priceless artworks, or to destroy it all, Falconer opts for the castle's destruction.

His decision may seem contrary to those of the male leads in Pollack's other films in that Falconer chooses death rather than life, but the contrary is true. His actions attest to his belief in the American fighting spirit. Like Turner's concern for the future, Falconer is also concerned for the future in his maintaining the principle of American aggressiveness even though it means certain death against overwhelming odds. Falconer could not surrender to the Germans any more than Jeremiah could leave the wilderness or Kilmer could leave Japan before completing his task. Falconer must destroy the castle and his soldiers in order to try to preserve the principle of his American way of life.

Significantly, two individuals are not the victims of the destruction—the writer and Therese, who is pregnant with Falconer's child. Life and the arts will continue. Falconer's concern for Therese's safety illustrates the sensitivity to others which is seen in others of Pollack's male leads, but it is most directly related to the Joe Turner–Kathy Hale relationship in *Three Days of the Condor*.

The impersonal and machinelike environment of Turner's New York City world is the tank and machine-gun world of war for Falconer and Therese. Both couples have very tentative relationships, and their impersonality directly relates to the environment. While Kathy's boyfriend is merely a voice on the other end of the telephone (a voice which we do not hear) Therese's husband is both present and agreeable to her love affair with Falconer so that he might have an heir. In the midst of war, impersonality is essential not only for a person's survival, but in this instance for the survival of the family name. We see that Falconer does care about Therese, and we see that he cares about the men in his unit as well; but such sensitivity to others makes Falconer vulnerable. When he and Therese are in bed, they are protected from the rest of the world only by a fine, transparent curtain. Like Pollack's other male lead characters, Falconer is physically aggressive and principled, and his sensitive concerns for others are tempered by his environment.

Alan Newell

The concern which Falconer shows in saving Therese's life is a direct parallel to the concern which Alan Newell has in saving Inga Dyson's life in Pollack's first film, *The Slender Thread*. The relationship between Alan and Inga is as tentative as that of other relationships in Pollack's films, and it also reflects the masculine aggressiveness and sensitivity of the other films.

Alan's link to Inga is the telephone, and his position as the aggressor is clearly seen in his communication with Inga. He tries to keep her on the phone so that her location can be determined before she dies from the overdose of pills which she has taken. While on the one hand Alan attempts to jar Inga's sensibilities through verbal aggression, he also speaks to her in soothing tones of concern which manifest his concern for her plight.

The strength which Alan shows is a strength of character. His world has become depersonalized like Joe Turner's world, but he yet upholds the principle of the fundamental importance of life. Like Joe Turner, Alan Newell will reap no personal benefits from his principled actions, yet he stands out as one individual who is willing to bear the burdens of another during a time when people are moving apart from each other.

Joe Bass

The environment of Joe Bass in *The Scalphunters* also provides examples of principled actions. Set in the arid climate of the early American West, *The Scalphunters* offers Joe Bass as a further example of an aggressive individual who maintains principles. His is a masculine world, though, of rough and tough men and women. Lacking Jeremiah's Swan, Turner's Kathy, Kilmer's Eiko, or Falconer's Therese, Bass's concern is first for his horse, and then for Joseph Lee in his gruff efforts to teach him the ways of the desert.

Although women travel in the scalphunters' caravan, Bass shows no more compassion for them than he does for the scalphunters themselves. He would just as soon start a rock slide down on top of their heads as he would send one down on the men. *The Scalphunters* is, after all, a comedy; one man's tender concerns for a woman could be only tentative at best. In spite of the comic overtures, Bass nevertheless shows as much compassion as any rugged individual in his position could show. He does not start the landslide without warning; he does not shoot to kill unless he has become the hunted first. But with Joseph Lee, Bass shows a concern which is as relative to his liking of him as it is to his ownership of him.

Since Joseph Lee was the by-product of an undesired "trade" with the Indians for Bass's furs, Bass first has an interest in him for his value on the auction block. Showing all the marks of the owner/slave relationship, Bass rides his beloved horse while Lee struggles on foot in his attempt to keep pace. When Bass agrees to change positions, we may first think that he is being humane and compassionate to the suffering Lee, but, alas, such is not the case. Realizing Lee's inclination to ride off on the horse, and also realizing that the horse will throw his rider at the sound of a whistle, Bass has his scheme planned ahead of time—further humiliation for Lee.

As the film progresses, Pollack begins to establish a growing bond between the two completely opposite individuals. Bass's concern for Lee in his capture by the scalphunters is ambiguous, though. Bass ostensibly desires only to regain his property, yet we well know that he is trying to free his friend as well. The scene at the end of the film summarizes both the aggressive masculinity and masked concern which Bass shows for Lee. They stand and slip in muddy water as they try to beat each other to a pulp, yet they ride off together on Bass's horse in their continued quest for the furs which are now back in the hands of the Indians after having been taken in between by the scalphunters.

Bass will begin tracking Two Crows again as a matter of principle. He could take Lee to the auction block and sell him for more money than he would earn from the sale of his furs, but he won't. In matters of ownership, and in matters of theft, what is his, is his. The purely logical action could also include his returning Lee to the Indians who had captured him, but such a response from Bass is dubious. As a second principled response, Bass would be most likely to save the life of one who had in turn saved his.

Bass would not simply be saving a life, but like other male characters in Pollack's films, he would be saving a way of life. He has had to kill individuals in order to protect his principles, but he has not destroyed others before they first attacked him. Bass will use all of his strength and aggressiveness if the situation warrants such action, but he remains fundamentally a calm individual who would rather seek the most peaceful solution to the dilemmas in which he finds himself.

Owen Legate and Robert

The same sort of peaceful solution to dilemmas is most poignantly seen in the films of the Depression, *This Property Is Condemned* and *They Shoot Horses, Don't They?* In the first, Owen Legate must decide whom to lay off, and in the second, Robert must decide if he should kill Gloria. The decisions for both characters would at first seem to be difficult, but within the context of the Depression Robert's choice to kill Gloria is more perfunctory than it is painful.

Robert and all of the individuals taking part in the dance marathon, both male and female, show a physical determination and assertiveness which speaks of the time period in which they are living. They may not kill each other with weapons, but they destroy others through their fierce determination to survive. The derby elimination races are more savage than the most brutal attacks which Jeremiah endured. The contestants shove, step on others, and elbow their way through to the finish. Those who have fallen are cheered, and the sailor who has died is not even mourned by his partner, Gloria. She is angry instead at having to find another partner before she too is eliminated.

Gloria's own death is even more clearly an image of the callousness of the times. Robert's willing compliance with her request to shoot her underlines, ironically, his sensitivity. The impact which Robert felt in his youth in seeing his grandfather shoot an injured horse never left him. He could not repress the memory of that event any more than he could overlook his recognition of the animallike treatment of people. Robert has no dilemma because he is so very perceptive of his surroundings. Robert does not destroy in order to preserve a way of life or life itself; he destroys because life has come to nothing for Gloria. As Robert is led passively into a cell which separates him from all others in society, Pollack offers an image of the reduced state of mankind which has been beaten into submission.

The contrast to Robert's character in *They Shoot Horses, Don't They?* is Rocky. As the master of ceremonies and apparent engineer of humiliation, Rocky seems the least caring of all of the characters in the film. His aggressiveness is verbal, like Alan Newell's, rather than physical as he attempts to keep the show going for as long as possible. While such objectivity seems to define Rocky's association with others, he too manifests a sensitive concern for others which is seen most poignantly in his attempt to ease the burdens of the crazed contestant Alice (Susannah York).

The point of *They Shoot Horses, Don't They?* is directly linked to Pollack's presentation of male characters like Rocky. They struggle to survive through conflicts which are particular to their world, and they show compassion for others which is tempered by the time period in which they live. The horror of this film is the horror of the time.

A second film of the Depression, *This Property Is Condemned,* also presents male characters who are typically aggressive and yet sensitive to others. Owen Legate lacks the physical assertiveness of the contestants in *They Shoot Horses,* but his character is tempered by the structure of the film. *This Property Is Condemned* is a narration of Willie's past. Legate was her idol, so his depiction on the screen is framed within either Willie's observations of him when he was in Dodson, or in her projected image of him when he was physically apart from her.

Appropriately, Willie details more of Legate's compassion than his aggression. As her savior, and as the only warm, human contact which she had in Dodson, Legate is seen primarily in his moments of tenderness with Willie and her sister, Alva. We see Legate as a direct contrast to the other men in town who are characterized by their insensitivity and animallike behavior. Legate attempts, for example, to lay off railroad employees without families first; and his interest in Alva goes beyond her sexuality as we see him asking questions of her past and attempting to provide for her future.

Legate is also remembered by Willie as an aggressive person, but the one act of aggression which she recounts shows his concern for her. The boys have been taunting Willie about her sister, and Legate pushes an ice-cream cone into the face of one of them. Willie's story is replete with the physical brutality displayed by the railroad workers, but her memories of Owen are the memories which Eiko would have of Harry Kilmer or that Janice would have of Joe Turner.

Owen Legate is depicted as the gentle kind of individual who survives because of his calm acceptance of life as it is. His rage is subdued perhaps through Willie's narration or perhaps by the times, but he will endure while others have failed. In many ways, Owen Legate is a transitional link to two others of Pollack's male characters who exist at the opposite extreme of a Jeremiah Johnson. While we may applaud the active pursuits of a Jeremiah or a Joe Turner, we in turn should pity the passive acquiescence of characters like Bobby Deerfield and Hubbell Gardiner. We have seen that the times can bring out the best in individuals, but Pollack also shows us that the times can subdue individuals to such an extent that they become almost completely unemotional; they are insensitive to those who are a part of their lives.

Bobby Deerfield

The story of Bobby Deerfield is the story of a boring individual who moves methodically through life with the kind of mechanical precision of his finely tuned race car. Any characteristic of aggression in Deerfield is directly linked to his race car.

Physical aggression plays no part in Deerfield's behavior. Even the throngs of spectators who surround him at the race track fail to bring any response from him. He calmly walks through the mobs without the slightest indication of any annoyance. If Deerfield is to assert himself, it is only through his race car. His physical effort is minimal as he turns the wheel, shifts through the gears, and depresses the accelerator. Deerfield's most calm and rational approach makes him a winner at the track, but it also makes him a loser in life in the sense that he is invulnerable to the sorrows around him.

Deerfield's visit to a hospital in order to visit a fellow driver who has been injured in a fiery crash exemplifies his invulnerability rather than his compassion. His concern is not for the health of his comrade but for the cause of the accident. For Deerfield, all is calculated and under control. The risks which he takes on the race track are minimal, and his own accident is the result of an unforeseen problem which could not have been predicted.

Deerfield figuratively destroys his competition so that he may preserve his own life-style. The difference between Deerfield and Pollack's other male characters is found in his pursuit of goals which are totally self-centered and totally materialistic. The principle involved is not man's right to be free or his right to own property, for Deerfield is without principle. As an individual almost void of emotions, he lacks the needed quality which would give him the strength to pursue an ideal. When Deerfield emerges into the light of day after his relationship with Lillian and her subsequent death, he is not substantively altered. He will not attack the "Indians" who were responsible; he will not look to his own failures in life. He will return to America, but not as Harry Kilmer returned from Japan. Deerfield's going home is as measured as his turn around the race track. As a product of the twentieth century, he has learned to protect both himself and his riches. His utterly cold, rational approach to life is the definition of his times, for he stands as the man who carefully measures his personal existence while giving little heed to those around him.

Hubbell Gardiner: The Fall into Aimlessness

The difference between Deerfield and Hubbell Gardiner in *The Way We Were* is seen in the way in which they are affected by the people around them. We can respect Deerfield's isolation since it shows a certain kind of strength in his pursuit of defined goals. Hubbell Gardiner, however, is as aimless as his drifting sailboat. He bends to the will of others with minimal understanding of either himself or his position in life. While Deerfield is at least at the wheel, Hubbell never mans the tiller.

Hubbell's complete lack of aggressiveness makes him the weakest of any of Pollack's male characters. He constantly moves according to the will of others, and his course through life is defined more by idle acceptance than by active pursuit. While all of Pollack's male characters are sexually aggressive—with the exception of Joe Bass and Alan Newell, who are not even physically close to women—Hubbell generally is not. When Katie first takes Hubbell to her apartment, and when the camera follows the trail of Hubbell's clothes into the bedroom, we find an inebriated man who is as impotent in bed as he is in life. He does later father a child, but both the child and the intimate encounters are unseen. We see only Hubbell's willing manipulation by others.

Hubbell shows aggressiveness in various sporting events in college, but in each he is responding to the will of others as Pollack intercuts shots of crowds of people urging him on. Hubbell never stands alone at the finish in the way that Pollack's other male characters stand triumphant in victory. Instead, Hubbell blends in with the very crowd that pushed him to victory. In the one instance when Hubbell does stand alone, after attacking a person who was taunting Katie for her support of the Hollywood Ten, he appears small in a huge hall beside Katie, and his bloodied face speaks more of his defeat than of his victory.

Hubbell's story is that of a man who has succumbed to the will of those around him. If he were unintelligent, we could accept his position as the pawn of others. He does have intelligence, though. He is capable of writing a moving story which gains a professor's praise, and he is capable of writing a book, *A Country Made of Ice Cream*, which is good enough to be published. Hubbell's complete lack of principles sets him in direct contrast to Katie while at the same time placing him at the lowest level of all of Pollack's male characters.

Hubbell can write, but he gives himself to Hollywood for all of its tinsel glamour and promises of immediate wealth. Hubbell can compete in Hollywood, but he chooses merely to agree so that he finishes with the pack rather than ahead of them. Hubbell can try to solve the problems of his marriage, but he lets it fall apart without taking any active measures which would ensure its continuance. Hubbell Gardiner is the image of America the Beautiful, but there is nothing behind the facade. He is not merely irrational; he is an unthinking and aimless individual who prostitutes himself to others for money and status.

The nature of the male characters in Pollack's films encompasses the range of human existence. Overall, Pollack tends to show individuals of principle and sensitivity who willingly place themselves in conflict in order to rectify wrongs or to ensure the continuation of life. Individuals like Bobby Deerfield and Hubbell Gardiner, however, illustrate levels of existence which are directly related to the growing materialism of their societies. Some men succumb while others maintain their principles. Had Deerfield lived in the time of Jeremiah Johnson, his most calculated assessment of his position in life would have made him a hero—perhaps a legend. If Hubbell had lived at that time, he would probably have maintained residency in the East! Any given time period brings out both the best and the worst in mankind, but the majority of Pollack's male lead characters are generally representative of the most admirable of men.

DENTIST
CREDIT DENTIST

6

The Inner Strength of Women

" . . . I think most of the women characters are quite strong. I'm interested in women as a director. I wouldn't want to do a picture without a strong woman's role. The women in my films have been stronger emotionally than the men; they have more perserverance, more wisdom" —Sydney Pollack

* *

Throughout Sydney Pollack's films, the male characters generally are the focal points in their struggles to cope with the conflicts which surround them. Whether Jeremiah Johnson defending himself against the attacking Indians, the soldiers of *Castle Keep* trying to save a castle from the enemy, scalphunters warring with Indians for their scalps, or race-car drivers battling with each other, the males exhibit an active strength of purpose which is denied most of Pollack's female characters. Yet the strength of the female leads in Pollack's films is not to be denied. On the one hand, and set most vividly in the Katie Morowsky character of *The Way We Were*, the Inga Dyson character of *The Slender Thread*, and Gloria of *They Shoot Horses, Don't They?*, Pollack presents women who defy the conditions which surround them. On the other hand, and in a more subtle manner, Pollack also presents women like Eiko in *The Yakuza* and Willie in *This Property Is Condemned* who possess a tenacious strength in their acceptance of life as it is. They are stronger than their male counterparts, for they are not defeated by the surrounding conflicts. The strength of both sorts of female characters is in their understanding of life as it is.

Katie Morowsky: Active Strength

The active strength of the Katie Morowsky character in *The Way We Were* comes closest to the active strength of most of Pollack's male

Photo: Ruby and Gloria strain to carry the unborn and the dead to the start/finish line in They Shoot Horses, Don't They?. *(credit: Movie Star News)*

characters. The difference is that Katie pursues a much broader cause than most of the male characters. Katie's husband, Hubbell Gardiner, passively accepts the conditions of his world, a point which Pollack implicitly states through his visual omission of Hubbell's active involvement in the war. Katie, however, is continually seen as an activist. Her belief in principles may set her apart from the majority, but she willingly takes a stand even though her position leaves her vulnerable to ridicule and abuse. While Katie continuously exemplifies her beliefs, Hubbell remains in the background. As a spineless manifestation of an individual who lives without any principles of his own, and as a representation of an individual whose principles are materialistic in nature, Hubbell is merely at one with the multitude.

Pollack offers visual evidence of Katie's strength and Hubbell's weakness throughout the film. Hubbell's life, other than his quest for material gain, is highlighted most by his sailing, a certain rudderless and aimless drifting. Katie, not pictured in a similar manner, or even in the boat for that matter, stands at the top of the ladder and at the top of the frame with Hubbell beneath her. She encounters conflicts, but exits unscathed.

Gloria

The same sort of active defiance of life as it is is also apparent in Gloria in *They Shoot Horses*. While the contestants in the dance marathon continue to run in the derbies and painfully attempt to remain standing, Gloria has the only active insight into the nature of life. Robert may be the partner in her death, but he does so without any genuine insight. He equates people with animals, but such an equation is childlike in comparison to the insight to which Gloria has come.

Other characters see life as it is, but they are incapable of or unwilling to do anything about it. Maintaining only the financial goal, they do not look into the catastrophe of life as it has become. The emcee continues, for he is being paid for his performance; judges continue, yet they too are being paid. Other contestants drag themselves on, for they are lured by the promise of $1,500. Only Gloria looks beyond the superficial promise of the pot of gold in her agonizing recognition of the level to which life has fallen.

Inga Dyson

The same depth of understanding also holds true for the Inga Dyson character in Pollack's first film, *The Slender Thread*. Inga, though, is more the victim of her own self-condemnation than is Gloria. Circumstances bring her to the final recognition of the immensity of the deceit which she has perpetrated on her husband, but she does not shun her responsibility. Rather, she is tormented by it until she, like Gloria, sees death as the only viable alternative.

Inga's strength is found in her complete acceptance of her guilt. While her attempted suicide may appear to be a coward's way out, such action is a definitive stand. It is not only a recognition, but an active response to the insight which she has gained. Such insight is not true of scalphunters, Hubbell Gardiner characters, or soldiers whose conscience allows them to carry on in spite of the atrocities which they have done to others. Inga's "crime" seems almost insignificant in comparison to others' literal or figurative slaughter.

The calm acceptance of life as it is, so much a part of Inga's character until chance forced her to make a definitive response, is the characteristic which is found within other women in Pollack's films. Theirs is a strength which is internal, a realistic strength which recognizes the surrounding horrors while coping with them. Such strength is optimistic, for it implies a belief in the future.

Three Pregnant Women: Ruby, Therese, Swan

As a contrast to Gloria in *They Shoot Horses,* the pregnant Ruby in the same film epitomizes a faith in the future. She, of all of the contestants, has a reason for dropping out of the marathon, yet she, of all of the other women contestants, continues. Primarily motivated by her husband's desire to continue in order to win the money, Ruby endures. Unlike Gloria, she calmly accepts life as it is; the knowledge does not stop her since she holds the future in her unborn child. The strength which she manifests is strength and determination to carry on in spite of her surroundings. While Gloria had no future and consequently sought a way out of her insane world, Ruby does hold the future within her. Her recognition of her responsibility, and her calm acceptance of life as it is, provide the motivation for her continued efforts to survive. Perhaps most central to that strength, though, is her identification with her husband. Characteristically, the crazed women in Pollack's films are either unmarried or separated from their husbands.

Pollack's films contain other pregnant women: Therese in *Castle Keep* and Jeremiah Johnson's Indian wife, Swan. Like Ruby, Therese survives the atrocities which surround her. Her survival promises a future in her unborn child.

Photo: Therese (Astrid Heeren), a survivor in *Castle Keep*, watches her husband approach the castle. *(courtesy of Columbia Pictures)*

The soldiers of *Castle Keep* illustrate a physical strength throughout the film. They actively pursue the enemy, and they die for the cause. Yet they are actually as aimless as such other male characters in Pollack's films as Robert in *They Shoot Horses* and Hubbell in *The Way We Were*. In *Castle Keep*, Clearboy unwittingly jumps into a moat, rescues an unoccupied Volkswagen, and traces circles in the snow. Captain Beckman, the art historian, destroys the works of art which he has so carefully worked to preserve. Retreating soldiers and conscientious objectors wander away from the battleground in a daze; the women in *Castle Keep* maintain a much more clearly defined purpose to their lives.

In a curiously oblique manner the women of the brothel are similar to Therese. Although they help the American soldiers by dropping molotov cocktails on enemy tanks, they endure while the American soldiers do not. Like Therese, they accept life as it is. They take a more active role in the destruction around them, although they lack the active intensity of the soldiers. Dressed in their finest clothes, they stand on their balcony, wave to the enemy, and drop homemade bombs on the tanks. They are both a part of and apart from the action.

The baker's wife in this same film also responds on a similar level. She does not participate in the destruction, but she too lives in the midst of the fury. She accepts Sgt. Rossi as a replacement husband since hers has gone off to the war, and with Rossi she continues onward in the daily routines of life. She produces bread and pastries while destruction rages about.

Ongoing work in a most uncertain environment is also typical of Swan, Jeremiah's Indian wife. She, like Therese and Ruby, is also pregnant; unlike them, though, she does not survive to give birth to the child who symbolizes the union of two distinct traditions.

The quiet strength of purpose of Swan's life is most like that of Therese. Her purpose in life is life itself. Raised in a tradition which defines her role as subservient to that of men, Swan calmly accepts her marriage to the white stranger Jeremiah. She goes with him, learns his language, works alongside him in building their cabin, prepares the food, and plays the rugged games that Jeremiah and their mute "son" enjoy. She accepts life as it is, and through her pregnancy would provide for its continuance.

Swan's death, unlike Ruby and Therese's survival, is a statement about the future of a country rather than about the future of mankind—a country in its infancy which is yet incapable of a unification of opposite traditions.

Lillian

The juxtapositions of two traditions is also important in *Bobby Deerfield*, but Lillian's death rather than pointing out conflict, sees the creation of life, the rebirth of Deerfield, as its product.

The same innate understanding of the forces of life which characterize other women in Pollack's films is also expressed in *Bobby Deerfield*. Lillian accepts not only life as it is, but also death as it shall be. Deerfield's calm state is unlike Lillian's, for it manifests an avoidance of emotional entanglement with life while Lillian's is a calm acceptance of all that life has to offer. Her acceptance, perception, and willingness to pursue all emotional possibilities define her strength.

Lillian's determination to live with the awareness of her pending death is perhaps Pollack's strongest statement about the tenacious inner strength of women. Others of Pollack's female characters have faced death as it occurs around them, and others have died, yet Lillian stands as the ultimate example of a woman who understands the worth and optimism of life itself. Although she does not bear a child in the literal sense, the life force which she transmits to Bobby Deerfield through her death is as significant an event. Through Lillian, Bobby Deerfield moves toward an emotional awareness of life.

Eiko: Calm Acceptance

Lillian's European identity is not particularly important, for her insight into life is not restricted to the borders of any country. Eiko, in *The Yakuza*, though, is more strongly representative of the calm acceptance of life which has become almost stereotypical for the Oriental woman. Eiko's life, with its movement through encounters of supposed and actual death, typifies her total acceptance of life as it is, and life as it must be.

Faced with the supposed loss of her husband, Eiko's acceptance of Harry Kilmer as a lover is similar to the action of the baker's wife of *Castle Keep*. Kilmer is the enemy, but he can provide the needed medication for Eiko's daughter, Hanako. The prolongation of her daughter's life takes precedence over concerns about Americans occupying Japan. Tanaka Ken's unexpected return from the war means that Eiko must live apart from him since he cannot live with a wife who has disgraced him through her living with the enemy. The difference between Eiko and Tanaka Ken is the difference between the acceptance of life as it is and the imposed standard of life as it should be.

Tanaka Ken, although bound to Kilmer for saving his daughter's life, is also bound to a tradition of honor in the family structure. Eiko's duties are not divided. Like Therese and the baker's wife, her duty is first to life itself. She will live with the enemy in order to preserve her daughter's life, and she will survive her husband's disgrace because her previous actions saved the life of her daughter.

Women in *The Yakuza*, like *Bobby Deerfield*, are the catalysts to masculine awareness of the primary importance of life itself. Bobby Deerfield is reborn through the death of Lillian, and Tanaka Ken is reborn through the death of his daughter. Her death intensifies the importance of life itself, and the renewed perception brings Tanaka Ken closer to Eiko. Significantly, the women in *The Yakuza* are the prime movers even though the many graphic displays of masculine strength throughout the film would seem to portray the men as the moving factors. Generally in Pollack's films, men bring death and destruction while women bring life and the insight into its nature.

Kate

The death and destruction which runs throughout *The Scalphunters* is readily apparent. Typically, though, the women do not take part in it. They are protected from it and even carefully moved into a separate wagon in the face of danger. Kate, a former prostitute who lives with Jim Howie, never lifts a rifle to take an active part in the destruction around her. She, like so many of Pollack's women, accepts life and the conditions which surround it. She may object to smelly scalps and Howie's chewing tobacco, but essentially she is content.

Kate lacks the calm refinement of Eiko or Therese, for her world is yet in its pioneering state. She takes along her brass bed, and she sings hymns on a Sunday morning in her covered wagon, but she also lives in a transitory state as the wagons move slowly from one encounter with death to another.

With Jim Howie's death, Kate must reevaluate her circumstances. In a manner which parallels Eiko's joining the enemy, Kate does the same as she looks up at the Indians and comments, "What the hell, they're only men." No other statement seems to make the point so clearly that her concern is for life. She will endure while the men around her die. She seems so crude, yet she is not so different from Eiko, Swan, the baker's wife, or Therese. All of them rise above the horrors which surround them because of their ability to see that the importance of life is life itself.

Kathy

As a further example of the same principle, Kathy in *Three Days of the Condor* lives in the same manner. Like Kate, Eiko, and the others, she is both a part of and apart from the death and destruction which have been such integral aspects of her world. Her entrance into that world through Joe Turner's forcible abduction of her makes her a most unwilling victim, yet she also takes life as it is. She stops fighting Turner, and she becomes a willing accomplice in his attempt to expose governmental corruption while she herself remains as far away from the actual fighting as she can.

In her final acceptance of the conflicts which life has to offer, Kathy is a twentieth-century refinement of the Kate and Swan characters of Pollack's films of America during the 1800s. Like the others, Kathy is supportive. The difference lies in the ending of the film. The other women have been separated from their male counterparts through death. Swan is killed; Jim Howie is killed. Kathy's movement away from Turner speaks more pointedly of the greater transience of relationships in the twentieth century, a certain mechanical operation which precludes the continuation of emotional involvement. Kathy's perception of this idea is keen. While she is not as callous as Kate in her acceptance of the Indians, she does accept encounters on a short-term basis. She will leave Turner and so resume her relationship with her boyfriend for perhaps another weekend of skiing.

The Starr Women

The unstable relationship of Kathy and Turner also has a parallel in Alva and Owen Legate in *This Property Is Condemned.* The women of the Starr family in this film, the mother, Hazel, and her two daughters, Willie and Alva, represent all of the levels of women's strength seen throughout Pollack's other films. Willie, with the quiet strength to accept life as it is, is the hope for the future. Like Eiko, Lillian, Swan, Therese, and others who sense all of the good and bad which life has to offer, Willie will move forward in life. She will survive and endure with her calm acceptance of all that fate has dealt her.

Hazel will endure also; she too sees life as it is; she takes an active stand like Katie in *The Way We Were* and Kate in *The Scalphunters*, but as an exaggerated example of a woman who occupies a completely self-centered position, Hazel will use every means at her disposal, including Alva, in order to assure her own financial security. Hazel's position in life is the most villainous of any of Pollack's women, and she finds her equal only among male characters like Jim Howie in *The Scalphunters* or the assassin Joubert in *Three Days of the Condor* in their unemotional destruction of others for financial profit.

The difference between Hazel and her daughter Alva is found in their varying degrees of conscience. For a time Alva will accept the wretched conditions of her life; like her mother she will actively use men in order to find a better way. Like Gloria in *They Shoot Horses* and Inga in *The Slender Thread*, Alva sees the futility of life. Alva's circumstances are most like Inga's, though, for she began her life with Owen Legate in New Orleans as Inga began hers with Mark Dyson: with the knowledge of past sins. Their heightened awareness and subsequent self-condemnation are attributes seen only in women.

An Active Understanding of Life

Alva's forced awareness of the realities surrounding her destroys her as it did Inga, Gloria, the hysterical pioneering mother in *Jeremiah Johnson*, and Alice, the aspiring actress in *They Shoot Horses* who loses her mind. The implication for all of these women is that they are weak because of their inability to cope with the events in their lives, but they also express an emotional response to life which Pollack denies his male characters. The male conscientious objectors in *Castle Keep* are similar, but they are passive individuals like Bobby Deerfield who do not actively confront life as Alva and other women characters similar to her do.

All of Pollack's women, then, illustrate an active understanding of life. Through their insight, they take one of three directions: a Katie Morowsky, who will actively defy the injustices which she sees; an Eiko, who will calmly move through life and in a quiet way ensure the continuance of life itself; and an Alva Starr, as a composite of the two, who will be destroyed because of her expanded level of consciousness. All of them share a concern for the continuation of life; those who are destroyed have become aware of the insanity of prolonging life in a pointless world of masculine destruction. The majority of Pollack's women characters do endure, and whether a Katie Morowsky, who remarries, an Inga, who survives her attempted suicide, or a Lillian, who is reborn through Bobby Deerfield, they will continue to express an insight into life which Pollack gives to few of his male characters. While Pollack's men destroy in their roles as the preservers of life, Pollack's women create for exactly the same reason.

7

The Question of Villainy

"In the book [Six Days of the Condor] the villain is a horrible, horrible man—a pure mercenary who kills strictly for money. He was the kind of mustache-twirling villain that just bores me. So we began to construct a man whose amorality was more solvent than the CIA morality. The Von Sydow character is an honest bad guy, which I prefer any day to a lying good guy. Now I'm not saying it's better to be a killer and admit that you're a killer than to be the CIA. What I am saying is that this man knows that economics determine who are the good guys and who are the bad guys, if there are any such things. Therefore he chooses to isolate himself from society and make his own morality. He relies only on his own excellence"

—Sydney Pollack[1]

* *

The appearance of villains in Sydney Pollack's films is an interesting one, for we are often deliberately confused about their identity. Individuals who are instruments of death are found in six of Pollack's films, yet they are not one-dimensional villains. Those who kill for money are villainous, but even they are developed so that we recognize a grain of goodness in each of them. Their benevolent attitudes not only make them more realistic as human beings, but also that much more horrifying in our forced recognition that any individual could well become the instrument of another's death if the circumstances were right. Whether killing by contract or killing by necessity, the "bad guys" in Pollack's films force us to question our understanding of right and wrong.

Photo: Max Von Sydow as Joubert, a most cunning villain in Three Days of the Condor. *(credit: Movie Star News)*

Indians

Pollack's two Westerns, *Jeremiah Johnson* and *The Scalphunters,* set in roughly the same time period in the subjugation of the American West, place the complex question of right and wrong before us. Through these two films we encounter deaths inflicted by Indians, whites, and a black; but even the most savage destruction of people is not always the worst in terms of our acceptance of it. The gradations of our judgment lie in our understanding of the motivation behind the killing, but they also lie in our recognition of some greater abstract and unprincipled force which has brought about the situation to begin with. All of this inevitably returns to Pollack's consideration of the human condition in general, but to the American condition in particular.

Generally, the Indians depicted in the westerns which first appeared on the screen were categorically the bad guys as they sought the destruction of the "palefaces" intruding in their domain. Pollack's films provide the same motivation in the most general way, but he adds a dimension to his characterization of Indians which makes their destructive acts more acceptable to us than the "palefaces'" destruction of them.

Paints-His-Face-Red in *Jeremiah Johnson* displays an attitude toward Jeremiah which is neither particularly benevolent nor malicious. In the opening of the film, Paints-His-Face-Red calmly sits on his horse as he watches the clumsy Jeremiah try desperately to catch a fish. He neither slaughters Jeremiah for his presence in the territory nor aids him in his efforts to survive. Nature will take its course. When Jeremiah later takes the military search party through the Indians' burial ground, the situation changes. Now Paints-His-Face-Red must, because of the disrespect which Jeremiah has shown in trespassing through the burial ground, destroy him. In taking action which results immediately in the deaths of Jeremiah's pregnant wife and muted "son," Paints-His-Face-Red has made a partial atonement to the spirits for the white man's intrusion.

The tribe's continued pursuit of Jeremiah brings another facet with it. They could well have killed Jeremiah easily by advancing on him as a group, but such was not their method. As Jeremiah had silently entered one of their camps and killed many of their tribe, so they silently advance on him, although only one goes each time. The attacker holds the upper hand, but the contest is even from the point of Jeremiah's discovery of his attacker.

The same sort of fair play is also evident with Jeremiah. His brutal slaughter of Indians is just that, but his motivation for the revenge of the savage annihilation of his family allows us to accept his act. His act of mercy in allowing one Indian to leave unharmed further complicates our attitude toward him. He is not merely unfeeling and ruthless.

Neither Jeremiah nor the Indians are one-dimensional characters. The question of right and wrong is unresolved even in the sign of peace which Paints-His-Face-Red and Jeremiah express for each other. Neither seems wrong. They are both motivated by principle rather than by greed. Both follow the dictates of conscience in furthering principles which are respected by others.

The principle changes in *The Scalphunters*. Rather than being concerned with the sacred dead and the sanctity of the family, we are forced to shift our concern to the importance of material goods. The movement provokes a more clearly defined understanding of that which is bad, yet even in this situation Pollack provides additional insight which points out elements of goodness found in apparent villainy.

The initial contact between Joe Bass and the Kiowa Indians has all the markings of the stereotypical one-against-many situations of the old Westerns, but the bad guys change color, so to speak, and turn the tables in this comic Western. Bass is trapped; he does not want to give the Kiowas his furs; his wishes are inconsequential. In a wonderfully comic situation in which the Kiowas defy all definitions of bad and good, they take Bass's furs and whiskey and then leave him with their unwanted captured slave, Joseph Lee, in trade. The difference between the tribes of *The Scalphunters* and of *Jeremiah Johnson* is the difference between conflict over principle and conflict over material goods. The Kiowas are not particularly good, but yet they are not particularly bad, either. Our additional knowledge that Joseph Lee was accepted as an adopted member of the Comanche tribe further complicates any preconceived notion that Indians in general are the bad guys.

The bad guys in *The Scalphunters* are the scalphunters themselves. With money as their ultimate goal, they capture Joseph Lee so that they can sell him on the auction block. With a bounty provided by the federal government in mind, they stalk Indians and slaughter them while they are hopelessly drunk on Bass's whiskey. Clearly, they are the bad guys—until Pollack provides another dimension to them through their association with the women who travel in their caravan.

Through the intervention of Kate, Jim Howie allows Lee to ride rather than walk. In another situation in which Bass has triggered a landslide down onto the caravan, we see Howie quickly placing the women in a safe position so that they will remain unharmed.

Throughout the film the emphasis may seem to be on the brutal and calculated atrocities which characterize the scalphunters since such actions are shown in quick but graphic detail, but Pollack continually provides us with the other side of their characters. While uncivilized to the point that they will strap a dead man's body to the seat of a wagon for a decoy, they will also show a primitive sort of respect for the women. They will not only protect them, but they will sing and dance with them as well.

The motivations for the killings which occur in *The Scalphunters* truly serve as a means toward a definition of good and bad. The Kiowa Indians launch an attack on the scalphunters with all of the same elements of surprise, but their motivation is not only revenge (acceptable) but the renewed possession of the furs which the scalphunters have taken from them (not so acceptable). Joe Bass also kills, but he never acts without first giving a warning. While his apparent concern for fair play may make him seem good, we are nevertheless aware that he is interested in having not only his furs back, but Joseph Lee as well. Even Joseph Lee kills, but we accept his action because he shows his mistrust of Howie and in so doing solidifies the bond between himself and Joe Bass.

The final confrontation between the Kiowas and the scalphunters, while Joe Bass and Joseph Lee are at the same time fighting each other, results in our recognition of the nature of villainy in the film. Of the band of scalphunters, the women survive while the men are killed. Joe Bass and Joseph Lee ride off together, and the Kiowas ride off once again with the furs, the spoils of their labors. As in *Jeremiah Johnson*, the survivors were those whose actions are inspired by principle. The question of villainy in *The Scalphunters* remains, though, for we are aware that the scalphunters pursued their trade as a result of the bounty offered by the government. Besides, how can a man who falls out of a brass bed in his covered wagon while wearing pink long johns be all that villainous?

Exploiters

While the United States Government's offering of a bounty for dead Indians provided the motivation for potential villainy in *The Scalphunters*, it also has an important role in the perpetration of evil by individuals in three others of Pollack's films: *This Property Is Con-*

demned, They Shoot Horses, Don't They?, and *Three Days of the Condor*. The difference between the Westerns of the early American settlement and the films of the Depression and of the post-Watergate years is found primarily in the focus given to the consideration of good and bad. While the Westerns offer groups of people for our purview, the others center more on individuals.

The films of the Depression, *This Property Is Condemned* and *They Shoot Horses, Don't They?*, center on persons who must play villainous roles if they are to survive while multitudes around them fail. Living in a world which has gone mad, both Owen Legate of *This Property Is Condemned* and Rocky of *They Shoot Horses, Don't They?* find employment at the expense of others.

Owen Legate is a businessman. His interest is in economics. In a time of the reduced shipment of freight, he must look after the railroad's economic interest and so lay off men. If Pollack were to present him strictly from the point of view of the men of Dodson, he could concentrate on scenes like the one which shows Legate being attacked, and he would also show an uncompassionate individual who approached his job in a perfunctory manner.

Pollack does not present such a villain. The point of view which he establishes is all-inclusive. We do not simply see Legate standing on a level above the workers in the railroad shop, but we view his entrance into Dodson as well. He, like any transient riding the rails, must jump from the freight train when he comes to town. He walks the streets of Dodson with the men he must later lay off, and he lives with many of them at the Starr Boarding House.

Legate has a job to do, but he is also compassionate. He first questions the foreman about the workers' families before making any decision about which men to lay off. The implication is that those with families will not be laid off first. Legate's concern for the underdog is most pointedly seen, though, in his befriending of Willie. As the homely kid sister of a beautiful and promising older sister, Alva, Willie is the loner. Owen Legate is the only individual who helps her ward off the insults of the town's young men, and he places himself on the line when he mashes an ice-cream cone into one of the boys' faces when the latter taunts Willie.

Further evidence of Legate's potential villainy could be developed in his seduction of Alva, but the probable situation is reversed. While the majority of the men in Dodson crave Alva's attention, Legate does not. He appears calm; he leaves Dodson when his liaison with Alva appears hopeless. Deceit is as absent from his character as it is present in Alva's. He has exploited no one for any more personal gain than he can derive from his salary as an employee of the railroad.

A situation in *They Shoot Horses, Don't They?* is almost identical. Exploitation would seem to be the name of the game for Rocky as the master of ceremonies of a dance marathon, but he, like Owen, is more the one exploited than the one taking the action himself.

Like Owen's platform above the railroad workers, Rocky's position is the same. Standing behind his microphone above the agonized participants, Rocky seems apart from it all. He goads them on, counts the hours, and sleeps while the marathon goes on through the night. He appears unmoved by the struggling mass of humanity before him—at least to the spectators on the sidelines.

Like our perception of Owen, though, our point of view of Rocky is widened by Pollack. We see him not only as the spectators see him, but also as the contestants view him as well. Rocky not only moves down from his platform, but he also moves with the contestants in their inner circle of hell and degradation. Alice's insanity is Pollack's most

Photo: Rocky (Gig Young) as the detached master of ceremonies in They Shoot Horses, Don't They?. *(credit: Museum of Modern Art/Film Stills Archive)*

graphic presentation of the compassion which is as much a part of Rocky as his apparent nonchalance. Rocky's concern for her is more than superficial as he walks fully clothed into the shower with her in his attempt to calm her. Rocky is the apparent machination of the dancers' destruction, yet the shifts which Pollack gives us in the point of view continually detail Rocky's humane qualities. He is at one time the scrupulously clean example of the perfectly objective master of ceremonies, but he is also the unshaven image of ordinary humanity.

Gloria's seduction of Rocky, like Alva's seduction of Owen, perhaps best illustrates the point of view which we are to take of an individual who is caught in a wretched situation which may simply be the best of all possible alternatives. The apparent exploiter has become the victim of another. Rocky is vulnerable; he has weaknesses. He is not as much the perpetrator of evil acts as he is the individual who has found a means for survival in a world in which survival is dubious at best.

Pollack could have developed the one-dimensional villainous quality in both Owen and Rocky by restricting the point of view, but he chose not to. Instead, he widened the point of view in order to reveal a compassionate side of both individuals. The camera shows us individual men who make a living at the expense of others, but it also brings us into their private worlds so that we can see their exploitation as well.

As Pollack moves to the 1970s with the film *Three Days of the Condor*, he continues to look at villainy. Perhaps as a representative of a society which has become dehumanized and almost completely impersonal, Joubert of *Condor* stands out as the most villainous of all of Pollack's characters. In spite of the apparently one-dimensional villainy of his character, Joubert is also developed just enough so that he is plausible to us.

Like Legate in *This Property Is Condemned* and Rocky in *They Shoot Horses, Don't They?* Joubert alone stands out as the villain. Although he may have accomplices, they work under his direction. The individuals who direct his actions are as obscure as the government which places a bounty on scalps.

The manner in which Joubert operates reflects an age of impersonality. While Legate inquires about the workers with families before he lays anyone off, and while Rocky tries to ease the burdens of a crazed competitor in the dance marathon, Joubert shows no compassion for his potential victims. He scratches the names off his list as methodically as he devises the means for his victims' deaths. He has a job to do; he does it.

Joubert's more human qualities appear only after his contract is fulfilled. Throughout *Three Days of the Condor*, Pollack has shaped Joubert into the most mechanical and methodical of assassins. In his predictability and his mechanical precision, Joubert is like the elevator door behind which he and Turner stand. His final encounter with Turner, though, not only is indicative of his impersonal nature, but also ironically illustrative of a human quality in his character. Having the perfect opportunity to shoot Turner at point-blank range after having been unable to kill him previously, Joubert does not. The contract has run out. He has no personal grudge against Turner. His new target has become his former employer, and he in effect has joined forces with Turner. As the two of them walk away from the scene of the killing, Joubert asks Turner if he can "drop" him anywhere. A play on words, yes, but also an indication of Joubert as something less than a ruthless, unsophisticated, and amoral villain.

In *Three Days of the Condor, They Shoot Horses, Don't They?*, and *The Scalphunters*, the potential villains share a similar materialistic motivation. No one individual destroys another without being financially rewarded for his efforts. *The Scalphunters*, a film of America's settlement, and the films of the twentieth century depict the potential villains as employees of some unseen others who have paid for the services. All of these films imply a direct link between government and those who are the victims of it.

War: The Unseen Villain

Pollack's only war film, *Castle Keep*, provides further evidence of individuals who find themselves cast as instruments of destruction as a result of governmental policy. The true horror of war, with its resultant effect on people, emanates from this film, for the soldiers, like so many others of Pollack's characters, gain nothing—not even their lives—at the end of the battle.

An attempt to find a villain in *Castle Keep* is nonproductive, for all of the characters who are pictured in this film exist in a dreamlike world which defies distinct definition. Major Falconer may seem more bad than good in his coveting of Maldorais's wife, Therese, in his apparent disregard for art treasures, and in his decision to destroy the castle itself, yet he is encouraged by Maldorais to seek Therese, he disregards art objects because he is stalking the enemy, and he destroys the castle rather than letting the enemy take it for their use as a fortress.

We may think little of Therese in her affairs with both Germans and

Americans, but no distinct sense of right and wrong comes from her actions. The Comte de Maldorais has approved of her actions as his only means to ensure an heir to his family. In fact, they are blood relatives. Therese may seek both German and American lovers, but she reacts with both sympathy and sensitivity to all of the men in her life.

The women of the Red Queen are similarly indefinable. Their brothel may at first seem unacceptable, but it provides a refuge from the fighting for the American soldiers. They may take the soldiers' money, although significantly such transactions occur off screen, but they are also willing helpers to the Americans as they toss molotov cocktails on enemy tanks—a further indication of their duality as the instruments of both destruction and love.

The soldiers themselves are perhaps most ambiguously portrayed. While we see the men of Falconer's unit in pursuit of the enemy and in the defense of the castle, we also see conscientious objectors who are unwilling to slaughter. The division in the ranks is particularly typical of Pollack in its providing more than a single dimension to a character or a group of people. Neither group of soldiers is wholly right nor completely wrong in its stand.

Of all of the scenes in *Castle Keep*, the Brahms "Lullaby" scene most sharply illustrates the nature of good and evil. In this scene, an American soldier plays a melody on a recorder while he is on patrol with others. A German soldier, hearing the melody from his hiding place, offers to play the "Lullaby" for the American so that he can hear the correct phrasing of the melody. While the hidden enemy instructs the American soldier in the subtleties of phrasing, he at the same time identifies his position. An American soldier shoots him as he hides in the bushes. Our response to the killing is almost indefinable. We recognize the German's position as an enemy, but we also see him as a willing teacher whose desire to help another outweighs his value for his personal safety. The crack of the rifle is a shocking contrast to the melodious lullaby, and the bloodstained recorder is a visual reminder of the conflict which makes little provision for harmony. The villain in *Castle Keep* is an unseen as he is in other of Pollack's films, for in this instance it is war itself.

Tradition and the Ambiguity of Villainy

The many conflicts which appear in *The Yakuza* offer further evidence of the disruption of harmony, yet the definitions of good and bad in this film are more complex than those seen in *Castle Keep*. With its setting in Japan, and with the establishment of a link between vengeance and honor, *The Yakuza* presents individuals who kill because of their obligations to others who have helped them. Rather than being exploited, they are willing participants who seek harmony through conflict.

Harry Kilmer's presence in Japan is directly related to war, but while *Castle Keep* shows aspects of it in the present, *The Yakuza* refers to it in the past. The horrors of the war are diluted through Wheat's narrative of the past while we look at present-day Japan, but we remain aware of the conflict which brought Kilmer and Eiko together. While they were on opposite sides during the war, the conflict brought harmony as Kilmer found the desperately needed medicine for Eiko's daughter. With Eiko's husband, Tanaka Ken, apparently lost in the war, Kilmer assumes his role and so recreates a family unit until the American occupation of Japan ends. Kilmer's ease in adapting himself to the Oriental life-style and philosophy further exemplifies the harmony which can grow from conflict. Aware of the Japanese code of *michi*, Kilmer accepts his responsibility to Eiko; before he returns to America, he ensures her financial future through his purchase of a business for her.

The likely villains of *The Yakuza* would at first appear to be the yakuza themselves since they operate in an underground world of gambling, drug dealing, and gun selling. Their abduction of George Tanner's daughter is made known to us early in the film, so our expectations of them would be expectations for any villainous group of individuals. As in Pollack's other films, though, our perceptions of them are broadened. We not only see other villainous types, but we also see the yakuza in terms of their Japanese tradition of honor.

The difference between our perceptions of the American group headed by Tanner and the yakuza has everything to do with Japanese tradition. The yakuza may seem more evil because of the size of their organization and the wide range of their criminal activity, but in a strange way, and bound to an old tradition, they are not as evil as the American group. Two of the yakuza back Kilmer into a corner in a lavatory, but they warn rather than maim. Their confrontations with the traditional swords are more poetic than they are repulsive, and the fluidity of their movements is both beautiful and awesome—both delicate and strong. The duality with the yakuza, then, is seen not so much in their activities as in their presence. They may well employ modern weapons and underwater knifings, but they are as much the delicate flower as they are the hardened steel.

Tanner and his men lack both the flower and the delicacy of movement. Their world is mechanical, and, unlike Kilmer, they are bound to no abstract concept of duty and obligation to others.

Kilmer's decision to go to Japan with Tanner in an effort to rescue Tanner's daughter comes from his sense of obligation to a friend. His knowledge of Japanese tradition and his acquaintance with Tanaka Ken, a former member of the yakuza, could well ensure the girl's safety. In his own way, Kilmer is the American embodiment of the Japanese tradition. The striking difference between him and Tanner is to be found in Tanner's deceit. Kilmer agrees to help Tanner, but he does not learn the true motive behind the kidnapping until he is in Japan. Tanner has accepted payment from the yakuza for weapons, but he has failed to deliver them. In essence, Tanner has violated his obligation to both the yakuza and Kilmer by being deceitful in both situations. His unprincipled actions seem more devious than the yakuza themselves.

In a refinement of the question of good and bad, principles and lack of principles, we are also aware of the relationship between Kilmer and Eiko. Considering the postwar period, the presumed death of Tanaka Ken, and Kilmer's sense of responsibility for Eiko's welfare, we can hardly call his living with her an unprincipled action. The perplexity of the situation comes later when we, and Kilmer, learn that Tanaka Ken is Eiko's husband and that he has moved apart from Eiko and his daughter rather than living with them and with the knowledge of Kilmer's past intrusion into his family. Eiko could not be deceitful; she had told her husband of Kilmer's life with her and of his saving her daughter. Yet Tanaka Ken's action remains ambiguous. We resent him for his inability to forgive, and we question his form of action, but at the same time we respect him for holding fast to the traditions which require him to respect those who have helped him and to shun those who have broken the responsibility borne of marriage.

Kilmer's response to Tanaka Ken's true identity is equally ambiguous. His act of atonement in cutting off his finger seems both wonderful and stupid. In helping Eiko after the war, in recreating a family unit, and in ensuring her financial future Kilmer seems worthy of our admiration. When the traditions of old enter in the person of Tanaka Ken, Kilmer's actions after the war appear less than admirable. The ambiguity remains. Our judgments of individuals are always tempered by Pollack's inclusion of a broadened point of view. Tanner's group, the yakuza, and the individuals associated with Tanaka Ken's family are all examples of the potential for good and bad within everyone, but the interpretation of the individual event is more a matter of tradition than personal inclination.

Pollack's films are no different from any other director's films in the relationship drawn between circumstance and resultant action. Pollack's difference lies in the enlarged point of view which he provides. His villains are multi-faceted; they show human frailties and they are often victims of unseen or intangible forces. It is a matter of focus. *They Shoot Horses, Don't They?* is not so much a film about a master of ceremonies who makes his living from the suffering of others as it is a film about the essential absurdity of life without meaning. *The Scalphunters* is not so much a film about the Indians and the whites in the settlement of the West as it is about man's unprincipled quest for money. *Castle Keep* is not so much a film about the horrors of war as it is about courage in untenable situations which have been created by a greater unprincipled force. In all of the situations, even with Joubert in *Three Days of the Condor*, Pollack gives the villainous types enough human qualities so that we can identify with them and so understand our own potential for villainy in similar situations.

8

The Electric Horseman

SINCE THE PREMIERE of *The Electric Horseman* on December 16, 1979, offers the opportunity to test the observations which have been made about Pollack's previous films, a final chapter on this film seems an appropriate conclusion to this book. The visual style, the structure, the implications about American traditions, the nature of the male and female characters, and the nature of villainy shown in *The Electric Horseman* offer further illustrations of Sydney Pollack's involvement in his films.

Visual Style

Attention to the visual aspect of *The Electric Horseman* is as careful as it has been in all of Pollack's other films. Continuing to use the screen image as a visual supplement to the theme, Pollack directs our attention to the artificial values of American materialism. The artifice of a materialistic existence is most graphically the electric horseman, Sonny Steele (Robert Redford). His movement from the essential darkness of Las Vegas to the brilliant light of day in the canyon in which he sets the racehorse Rising Star free is Pollack's visual treatment of the central theme of the film.

Over all, *The Electric Horseman* is literally a very dark film. Such darkness is in part a by-product of filming in Caesar's Palace, but Pollack carries the darkness outside in his filming either at night or on dull, cloudy days for much of the movie. The light which we do see in Las Vegas, with its dazzling displays along the Strip and its electrified "stars" in the ceiling of Caesar's Palace, is necessarily as artificial as the materialistic values contained within. Lighting is designed in casino halls so that the gambler has no sense of night or day; Pollack uses the same technique metaphorically to create Sonny Steele's mood until he

Photo: Hallie Martin (Jane Fonda) and Sonny Steele (Robert Redford) about to free Rising Star in The Electric Horseman. *(courtesy of Columbia Pictures)*

sets Rising Star free in an active declaration of his renewed sense of the fundamental importance of freedom over materialism.

Like the garish lights of the casinos which illuminate the Strip, all that Sonny Steele represents with his electrified and pulsating cowboy outfit can only be fully realized in darkness. Pollack's first presentation of Sonny as the electric horseman emphasizes the creation of an illusion which is both artificial and gaudy. We initially see Sonny as his companions try to sober him up before leading him to his horse. Sitting in a dimly lit room with gray lockers for a background, Sonny is a pathetic figure as he is pulled to his feet and helped to his horse. The high-school football fans clap and roar with delight as the field falls into darkness and Sonny rides in with the lights of his outfit aglow. The illusion of his brilliance is sustained, but then Sonny falls flat on his back and so destroys the illusion. With such an opening, Pollack has given us both the level and the darkness to which Sonny has fallen. The progression from this point will be measured in Sonny's attempt to rise out of his situation as he parallels Rising Star's movement to freedom.

Whether endorsing Ranch Breakfast in a shopping mall, riding a mechanical horse in a supermarket, or sitting in on an Ampco press conference in a room at Caesar's Palace, Sonny exists in a world of darkness and artificial light. He is lit by neon, flashbulbs, and reflected light from slot machines, but he is also illuminated by commercialism itself.

Sonny appears in the convention hall, where product displays attempt to capture the interest of potential customers. He is not only present in person, but he is also present as a cardboard cutout with all of the appropriate lights flashing. As Sonny stands in a strained conversation with one of the Ampco executives, though, he is positioned next to a display of motorcycles. Signal lights flashing, the motorcycles go around in circles while scantily clad girls ride them to nowhere. Each time a motorcycle passes Sonny, it reflects a pulse of light on his face as a visual indication of his position in the materialistic world which surrounds him.

Sonny's position in life is also shown when he is riding in a mirrored elevator in Caesar's Palace. We look at him standing in half-light as the camera pans up from his glittering boots to his ornate hat, but our attention is drawn to the thick electric cord which is wound around his hand. Sonny is larger than life as he and his reflected image fill the dimly lit frame, but we cannot escape the glittering materialism

Photo: The duality of Sonny Steele, grasping an electrical chord, his source of power. *(courtesy of Columbia Pictures)*

around him which has reduced him literally and figuratively to a cardboard-cutout individual. When we see Sonny push the red emergency button in the elevator, we see the end of his services as yet another of Ampco's products.

Sonny's decision to do something about himself and Rising Star is seen in his spectacular ride off the stage and through the casino, yet he still moves in a world of semidarkness. With the lights of his outfit blinking, he moves out of the casino and into the Las Vegas night. He blends with the animated lights which flash from numerous casinos, and he stands as the human version of the electrified image of a man shown outside the Pioneer Casino on the Strip. Sonny's exit from Las Vegas is striking, but when he unplugs his suit he plunges into darkness and disappears from sight as the sound of Rising Star's hooves echoes through the night air.

While we might expect to see Sonny next in the bright light of the rising morning sun, we do not. Sonny remains in half-light. We see him rise from behind a gray boulder which dominates the frame. His blue and purple outfit with its sequins and tiny lights is a gaudy contrast to the subdued browns and grays of the environment which surrounds him.

Sonny's first meeting with Hallie Martin (Jane Fonda) is also visually indicative of his lack of any substantive progress. While he is no longer illuminated by flashbulbs and spotlights, his campfire casts but little light on their nighttime encounter. Hallie's interest in Sonny is like Ampco's interest, and until she adopts his sense of what is right rather than what will bring in money, their journey together is filmed in the half-light of cloudy days and twilight.

The instances in which we do see the brightness of the full sun occur in two ways: in the visual contrasts to Sonny's position, and in instances of Sonny's most active defiance of Ampco. Through the beginning sequences of Sonny's escape with Rising Star, we become accustomed to his world of half-light and darkness. When Pollack intercuts a scene of Hallie's speaking in front of Caesar's Palace, we are stunned by the brilliance of the sunlight reflected off the front of the white structure. Hallie is the only individual who is clever enough to find Sonny, but the sunlight which she begins to share with him becomes the image of their defiance of all that Ampco represents. She secretly films Sonny's explanation of Ampco's mistreatment of Rising Star, she assists in Sonny's escape from the motorcycle "roundup," and she stands with him in the magnificent natural sunlight which permeates the canyon where Rising Star is freed. Each of these scenes is a direct contrast to the artificial lights of the casinos and rooms which have characterized Sonny's past existence.

Our final view of Sonny Steele presents conclusive visual evidence that he has broken all of his ties with materialism. We are well aware of the tangible differences since Sonny is now hitchhiking instead of riding in his white Cadillac convertible, but the camera movement shows us as well. With a helicopter shot similar to the one used in *This Property Is Condemned* in which we move fluidly from a close-up of Alva to a very high shot which looks down on her moving train, we move from Sonny's level and rise gradually into the sky while moving in a circular direction. The freedom which a helicopter shot shows for Alva is freedom for Sonny as well, but Pollack moves one step further. With an equation drawn between Sonny's movement from darkness into light, the camera itself, like Sonny, becomes the rising star. Sonny does not exit in the light of a brilliantly cloudless day, but he has at least moved away from floodlights, flashbulbs, and animated caricatures created in lights to advertise a world of illusion.

After having looked at the eleven films which Pollack has directed, we can say without a doubt that he gives meticulous attention to the details which form the image on the screen. Whether through the uses of the camera or through the selection of locations, props, and costumes, all that appears on the screen serves as a complement to the central themes found within the script.

Structure

The structure of *The Electric Horseman* is one of Pollack's least complicated in terms of logical chronology and manipulation of time. While Sonny Steele's rise to success as a rodeo champion is filmed rapidly through a montage which blends his series of achievements, his movement from his subservient position as a corporate tool to freedom occurs in less than a week. With the focus on his decision to save a magnificent horse and to reorder his life in the process, the nonessential events which have brought him to that point are deleted. In spite of the strict chronological time sequences, the film remains a circle like Pollack's previous films in that the end once again brings us back to the beginning.

The opening sequences of the film set Rising Star and Sonny Steele as the central characters. Our initial view of Rising Star shows him as a free-spirited animal lacking any constraints. The next scenes of

Sonny's participation in rodeo events imply a connection between Rising Star and him, although the two remain separate. In both situations, though, the one, rather than the many, stands out. Both are apart from the others around them as each displays a spirit which is particular to him.

The circumstances which brought Rising Star to such prominence that he would be bought by Ampco as a symbol of their corporation are as unimportant as the circumstances which made Sonny feel it necessary to sell himself to the same corporation as a symbol for their breakfast cereal. It is like the unseen span of time for Robert in *They Shoot Horses, Don't They?* after he has seen his grandfather shoot a horse and then recalls the event while on a Pacific beach. The important difference between these two films is that Robert's recollection provides a clue to what he is while Sonny's past speaks of what he was.

While Sonny may try at times to think of himself as a champion rodeo star, he is reminded that others can easily take his place in the darkness as they ride around the field in an exhibition of commercialism. Pollack filmed events from Sonny's past in slow motion, but even in slow motion they take such little time that they seem insignificant to his position as a promoter of Ranch Breakfast. Even Hallie, as the intense reporter who should have the facts, thought that Sonny had achieved the all-around championship only three times rather than five.

Pollack's structuring of time for the scenes which show Sonny's position as a corporate tool makes them seem to last longer than they actually do, for we are watching the painful process of his feeble attempt to do his job for Ampco. We see Wendell (Willie Nelson) and Leroy (Timothy Scott) practically drag Sonny to his horse before his display at the high-school football game; we see Sonny in his agonized effort to recall his speech in a shopping mall; and we see him riding a mechanical horse for an uncomfortably long period of time. The transitional links between these scenes which show Sonny's movement from one location to another in his open Cadillac are rapid, but then we once again must labor with Sonny in his performances.

By the end of the film, events begin to repeat themselves so that the end takes us back to the beginning. Rising Star is set free to run with the other horses, as we first saw him in the beginning, and Hallie and Sonny have a mock battle which is similar to their initial encounter in the wilderness. When Hallie leaves Sonny, she will return to her duties for the television station. She has been affected by her relationship with

Sonny, yet she remains essentially the same. Sonny's position is the same as well. We could hope that Sonny and Hallie would begin a life together, but their relationship is not to endure any more than any other male/female relationship in Pollack's films. Sonny was on his own as a rodeo star—no one could help him once he entered the ring—and he is on his own at the end of the film as he attempts to hitch a ride. A car goes by and then continues on its way without stopping to pick him up.

All of Pollack's films are circles. We may see a rapid series of flashbacks at the end of *Castle Keep* or be reintroduced to characters seen in the beginning of *Jeremiah Johnson*, but the end is always the beginning in some way. Even if the structure of the film does not literally take us back to the beginning, though, our perceptions about the main character do provide the circularity, for the characters remain fundamentally the same. We have seen them move through situations which have affected their lives, but the situations merely highlight character traits which they have always possessed.

The American Tradition

Money. The American tradition as seen in *The Electric Horseman*. In this film more than in any of his others, Pollack centers his concern on the materialistic values which typify the American way. The instability of the family unit also appears in this film as it has in the others as we see people coming together for only the most tentative relationships.

With Las Vegas as representative of American values, we are immediately made aware of the force at the very root of people's existence. While materialism is one aspect of most of Pollack's other films from the bounty paid for scalps in *The Scalphunters* to killing for money in *Three Days of the Condor*, he has not previously shown so graphically the effects which money has on individuals. The strongest allusion previously made was in another Redford role as Hubbell Gardiner in *The Way We Were*. With Ampco and its representatives as the focus for big business, we see the deception and perpetration of illusion which they foster on the American public.

The world of Ampco is exaggerated by its placement not only in Las Vegas but in Caesar's Palace—one of the more ostentatious casinos on the Strip. Pollack takes us beyond the plush interiors of Caesar's, though, so that we can see all of the tangible trappings of wealth. Sonny drives a Cadillac convertible, Ampco executives fly on corporate jets, limousines carry executives to their destinations, and Hallie wears the expensive and fashionable tight jeans and boots of the time. But like one character's comment about drinking, the people exist in "the world of illusion." Corporate jets and limousines eventually carry executives to Rim Rock canyon and to a real world of snow, ice, and an illusion created by Sonny about finding Rising Star; and Hallie stumbles and falls through the rocky terrain in fashionable attire which is more appropriate for the illusory world of Las Vegas than for the real one. Yet the executives and Hallie return to their world of illusion. Ampco will find another cowboy who is more than willing to endorse one of their products for an appropriate amount of money. It doesn't matter if he is likely to use the product, for as one of the executives has said, "You must not apply logic to advertising." Hallie also returns to her television news reporting so that her image can be projected into the homes of her viewers without their ever knowing that "Hallie" is really "Alice."

When Hallie became Alice, Sonny became Norman, but their real identities do not emerge until they spend time together away from the illusions of modern America. They do not reveal their identities until they leave not only Las Vegas but even their camper truck behind as they walk with Rising Star and sleep on the ground or in a wilderness cabin lit by a kerosene lamp and a fireplace. Their eventual separation is predictable, and it is one of the many separations of family units in this film as in Pollack's other films.

Sonny is characteristically a loner like others of Pollack's central characters. We have a glimpse of his origins in the opening of the film as we see him place his belt-buckle trophies on a table with a picture of a woman who is probably his mother, but neither she nor any of his family appear. Sonny lacks the solidarity of a strong family background as Deerfield, Jeremiah, and all others have. Even when Sonny is gaining status as a champion, he is alone. While the original script calls for a scene in which Sonny tosses his newly won belt buckle to a pretty girl who sits in the stands with his previously won trophies in her hand, we see no such scene in the final version of the film. Sonny is denied a close family relationship even with Charlotta (Valerie Perrine), his former wife.

We do see Charlotta and Sonny together, but their conversation is about separation and divorce. We realize that Sonny does not want to sign the divorce papers—he has been avoiding Charlotta while she is at Caesar's Palace—but such is his fate. Sonny never takes the wedding ring off his finger, but he is not to have a stable marriage, either. Our insight into the marriage of Sonny and Charlotta is fragmented, but our basic understanding of it is characterized by two isolated individuals rather than by a unified couple. We are not given hints about the solidarity of the couple; instead, we hear of Sonny's bringing home several cowboys so that Charlotta has to prepare food for all of them, and of Sonny's back-seat affairs while he is married to Charlotta.

Other stable family units are also missing from the film. Hallie makes mention of her sister, but only to explain the origin of her name. Wendell and Leroy travel with Sonny, but they speak only of women to be bought and not of wives. Even potential family units in the wilderness are incomplete as we see only individuals instead of whole families at various outposts along Sonny's trek to the canyon.

In spite of such depressing isolation, points of optimism do occur in the film with individuals who are willing to take a chance in order to help Sonny in his attempt to beat the system. In a way like Kathy Hale in *Three Days of the Condor*, Kay A. Bundy scorns the $50,000 reward, loads Sonny, Hallie, and Rising Star into his trailer truck, and takes them to safety out of the county. We hear a radio call-in show conversation in which others verbally join Sonny and Hallie in their defiance of Ampco and big business in general, but we cannot help wondering how many of them actually would have helped Sonny instead of taking the reward money if they had been given the opportunity. Even Bundy begins to feel doubts when he is questioned about the reward.

Ampco's decision to free Rising Star would also seem to be optimistic as well, but Pollack has been careful to provide their motivation. With sales increasing and T-shirts of Sonny being printed as a result of his escapades, Ampco tries to capitalize on the horse's release by publicizing the event and turning it into a promotional gimmick. The American way: increase sales and make more money in any way possible.

The Electric Horseman reaffirms everything that Pollack has been saying in his previous films about a lack of solidarity in the American way of life. America is continually shown as a composite of warring factions. Those who emerge victoriously do so only at the expense of others. America came into being as a result of groups of divergent people deceiving and destroying the Indians who occupied the land, and the American family as a metaphor in Pollack's films does the same. Although individuals establish family relationships, they never endure. Parents of central characters may be spoken of or implied through pictures, but they are never seen in person. It is as if we are looking at the highest block in a stack of building blocks without seeing the foundation. When Pollack takes us back to the foundation of America itself, he shows us further instability and isolation of individuals whose very existence is assured only as long as they are capable of destroying others.

For Pollack, as seen through his films, America is a country of divergent people who fail to come together in any solidified whole. While Pollack offers a note of optimism in his recognition that individuals like Katie Morowsky in *The Way We Were*, Joe Turner in *Three Days of the Condor*, and Sonny Steele in *The Electric Horseman* are willing to fight the system, we are yet aware that they must pay a price for their actions since they exist apart from the mainstream of American life.

The guiding principle of America, its tradition, is centered around the quest for money. Scalphunters collect their government bounty, dancers in a marathon suffer degradation for the possibility of winning $1,500, mothers use their daughters' attractiveness as a means to financial security, and writers sell their talent to Hollywood at the cost of their integrity. With *The Electric Horseman*, Pollack brings the money-grubbing tradition into its sharpest focus, yet he offers the insight that all do not remain caught in the trap of commercialism. At least one individual discards all that Las Vegas represents even though his actions place him on the side of the road. Sonny Steele, like America, has nothing to fall back on. The active strength and agility which made him a champion have been consumed until he has become merely a cardboard figure. Metaphorically, the active strength which brought America to the top in its position of power is also consumed as it broadcasts its monetary strength in bright lights from the facades of Las Vegas casinos. Seen in the context of Sydney Pollack's previous films, *The Electric Horseman* is a very dark film.

The Hero: Sonny Steele

The nature of the role which Robert Redford plays as Sonny Steele seems almost a composite of all of the roles which he has acted under Pollack's direction. Sonny Steele has the aggressiveness of Jeremiah, the perceptive qualities of Joe Turner, the sensitivities of Owen Legate, the athletic skills of Hubbell Gardiner, and the literal and figurative cardboard-cutout status attributed to Hubbell. Sonny's movement throughout the film is first that of Hubbell's, for he seems to take over where Hubbell has left off.

The difference between the opening sequences depicting Hubbell Gardiner in *The Way We Were* and Sonny Steele in *The Electric Horseman* is simply a difference of environment. Since Hubbell's world is that of East Coast Ivy League academia, he races sculls and mingles with the people who would frequent such an environment. Hubbell's college activities would be the same whether he lived in the 1930s, 1950s, or 1970s. Sonny's world of rodeo competition is also particularly suited to his western environment. Raised in an atmosphere in which men can test their athletic abilities against animals, he is as much a champion in the western world as Hubbell is in the more refined eastern world. They are both successful; they are both adored by the fans who surround them.

While both characters share the same kind of physical strengths, they also share the same vulnerability to business propositions which will make them wealthy. Both sacrifice the integrity which they may have had in the positions which they reached. Hubbell uses his writing ability as a means to Hollywood money, and Sonny capitalizes on his success as a rodeo champion so that he makes a mockery of his former status. The difference between Hubbell's drinking and Sonny's drunkenness is a matter of the level of consciousness which is raised. While Hubbell can blend in with the mainstream of nameless others whose paths of life parallel his own, Sonny is continually confronted with himself in the many forms which Ampco's advertising takes. But when he sees another man riding in his place without anyone in the audience realizing the deception, Sonny is forced to look at his position as a nonentity.

Sonny's change in attitude and resultant change in behavior bring with them characteristics like those seen in Jeremiah Johnson. Jeremiah's movement into the wilderness was as principled a movement as Sonny's riding off the stage at Caesar's Palace. While they both place themselves in positions in which they are one against many, Sonny's position is most like Joe Turner's in *Three Days of the Condor* since he is fighting a sophisticated network of people who have sophisticated machines to help them. With a setting more like Jeremiah's than Turner's, Sonny will be physically aggressive in his attack on the unseen figure who trespasses near him even though it turns out to be a woman.

As a parallel, though, Sonny is as tough on Hallie as Turner is on Kathy, although the relationship which Sonny has with Hallie is a blend between Turner-Kathy and Jeremiah-Swan. Swan is expected to carry her share of the load and does so since she has always been a part of the rugged wilderness. Similarly, Sonny expects Hallie to carry her share of the load—and perhaps rightfully so since Sonny insists that she carry only the trappings of her profession as a television journalist. She is a ludicrous figure in her attempt to keep pace with Sonny as she carries her heavy cameras and stumbles along in her high-heeled boots. When Sonny tosses the equipment into the river, he has removed the objects of his scorn. He then begins to react to Hallie with the sensitivity that Jeremiah displays for Swan and Owen Legate displays for Alva Starr.

Sonny is first drawn to Hallie as Joe Turner is drawn to Kathy. The four of them are fugitives, and the two couples almost desperately cling to each other in the fulfillment of their individual needs. New York City is not Utah, though, so Turner and Kathy cannot discard the objects which symbolize their way of life. They are surrounded by them.

While Sonny would not let Hallie put her film equipment on Rising Star, he does offer to let Hallie ride after her cameras have been discarded. The extent of his concern is shown in his holding out his cupped hands so that she can step up to mount the horse. We have previously seen evidence of Sonny's interest in women as characterized by Lucinda (Sarah Harris) at the supermarket where Sonny rode his mechanical horse, but he didn't even recognize her although they once spent a night together. With Hallie, or more particularly, "Alice," Sonny shows a genuine concern for her welfare much like Owen's concern for Alva or Jeremiah's for Swan.

The crossovers between the character of Sonny and other characters which Redford has played under Sydney Pollack's direction are apparent, yet Sonny's character is also like that of other male leads in Pollack's films. His total commitment to the action which he initiates is similar to the Burt Lancaster characters of Joe Bass in *The Scalphunters* and Major Falconer in *Castle Keep* and to Harry Kilmer (Robert Mitchum) in *The Yakuza* and Robert (Michael Sarrazin) in *They Shoot Horses, Don't They?* Sonny's total commitment is also his comparison to Bobby Deerfield (Al Pacino) with respect to Deerfield's total involvement with racing. Although all of Pollack's male characters in lead roles make commitments to situations which they follow through on,

Sonny is the first to walk out of a responsibility which he has undertaken. Yet his strength of character is even more pronounced as he changes his position to one which bespeaks his integrity rather than his weakness for money.

The Heroine: Hallie Martin

Similar to the crossovers in the characters which Robert Redford has played for Pollack, Jane Fonda's role as Hallie Martin bears marked similarities to her role as Gloria in *They Shoot Horses, Don't They?* Both characters are independent and perceptive individuals who display an aggressive quality which depicts their strength as individuals who will not be subservient to men.

Our first view of Hallie is as deceptive as she will prove to be to others. Standing quietly in a corner of an elevator at Caesar's Palace, she at first seems an unimportant and passive individual who is not a part of the action. Not so! This is merely one aspect of her character, one which tells her that there are times when she can gain more through her silence than through her speaking. Hallie's first confrontation with Sonny at the press conference shows her other side.

While reporters either ask questions about Ampco's impending merger or inane questions which ask a movie star to name the best kisser, Hallie immediately moves to a question about Sonny's late arrival to the meeting and then to a question about the possibility that he is deceiving the public in his endorsement of Ranch Breakfast. Like Gloria's denunciation of the pregnant contestant in the dance marathon, Hallie is quick to denounce hypocrisy when she sees it.

Hallie succeeds in locating the missing Sonny when all others fail because of her directness, but also because of her cleverness. People should be suspicious about her raising questions about Sonny's friends, but they are not, so Hallie gains bits of information which she needs to find Sonny and Rising Star.

Sonny should also be suspicious about Hallie, and he is. While she has called her television station in order to get film coverage of the release of Rising Star, Sonny has planned ahead in order to subvert her plans. The aggressiveness which characterizes Hallie is that of Gloria and that of Katie Morowsky in *The Way We Were* as well. She will succeed in her mission because of her aggressive qualities.

Hallie shows the tenacity, the inner strength to continue, which has characterized almost all of Pollack's female leads. While faced with numerous blockades in her pursuit of Sonny, Hallie never gives up.

Even if the pursuit of her goal means that she will have to suffer degradation, she will continue. She will take her equipment in spite of her having to carry it herself, and she will continue to trek through the wilderness even though she is ill-equipped to do so. The independence which is so much a part of Hallie is like that of Katie Morowsky, Lillian in *Bobby Deerfield*, Kathy Hale, and Eiko. While they love and are loved, they can also manage very well on their own.

If Hallie has any weakness, it is only in her willingness to scrap her whole plan to film the release of Rising Star. Even this weakness is a strength, for she is perhaps placing her job on the line for the sake of the principle involved. Hallie's priorities become like Eiko's in her turning to the enemy in her attempt to save her daughter, Hanako; like Therese's in her desire to bear a child; and like Kathy Hale's in her giving aid to her abductor. All of them reevaluate their positions when they must make decisions concerning the quality of life. The men in their lives may serve as the catalysts to their actions, but the women characteristically adopt positions which show their active commitment to the principles of life itself. Only when that principle has lost all meaning as in Pollack's films of the Depression and in *The Slender Thread* does the woman translate her perceptions into self-destructive action.

Generally, Pollack's female leads show a tenacity and inner strength which points out their endurance. Hallie is no exception. She, like so many of the women in Pollack's films, is affected by the surrounding conflicts, but she is not destroyed by them. Hallie will never completely lose her integrity in the way that Sonny did, for Pollack's women characters do not endorse products, kill Indians for their scalps, sell out to Hollywood, or engineer financial schemes which will bring destruction in their wake. Hallie may try to deceive people as others of Pollack's female characters have deceived those around them, but she does so in order to preserve a quality of life instead of destroying the very quality of life itself. Pollack's female lead characters are strong individuals. They will endure while others fail because of their strength of purpose in life.

The Villain?

We roar with delight as Sonny Steele makes a catastrophe out of a Las Vegas stage show, steals a $12 million horse, makes Utah policemen look like a modern-day version of the Keystone Kops, and effectively destroys a multi-million-dollar merger between two giant corporations. Then there's Ampco, which with materialistic deliberation and deception reduces people to nonentities. But then there's Hallie Martin, who under the pretense of goodness and helpful assistance is following a story which will boost her public image. They are all potential villains of *The Electric Horseman,* but they are not to be developed as such in a Sydney Pollack film.

Hallie has all of the necessary components to be a villain. She listens in on conversations; she verbally attacks Sonny's credibility in a press conference; she manipulates Leroy, one of Sonny's companions, so that she can track Sonny down; she films Sonny without his knowledge; and she attempts to make a media event out of the release of Rising Star in a betrayal of Sonny's apparent trust in her. Such character traits could well be developed so that Hallie would be little more than an evil force working against Sonny, but Pollack does not create such characters.

While Hallie does in fact perform multiple misdeeds, she is not the "bad guy." She may at first appear villainous in Sonny's eyes since she appears to be trying to thwart all of his efforts, but the professional interests which brought her to Sonny in the beginning make her progressively more of an ally than a foe in uncovering the deceptions of big business. She may first seem as tough as any cowboy when she swears at Sonny and belts him in the face, but such traits give way to our view of her as a rather vulnerable individual. As a result of her growing understanding of Sonny's purpose, and as a result of her human weakness for handsome men, she confesses her "villainous" past and joins Sonny in the spirit of his task. Hallie is neither a villain nor a heroine; she is as much a hindrance as a help, and she still uses her experience with Sonny as part of a televised report. It's good for her career.

Sonny's career as a world-champion rodeo star which we see at the beginning of the film has all of the necessary ingredients to make him a hero. As a handsome cowboy with all the requisite skills of his profession, he is admired by all. Then Pollack abruptly shifts the image so that we see the drunken remnants of a former hero. Sonny's status has changed, and he begins to take on negative attributes which summarily dash any conceptions which we might have held about his position as a hero.

His decision to steal Rising Star could well be indicative of the depths to which he has fallen, yet Sonny is no more of a villain than any of Pollack's other characters who might hold the same potential. We understand Sonny's motivation; we understand the principles behind his actions; we begin to see him as a hero in a different way.

Sonny does begin to take on heroic proportions again as he defies the values set forth by Ampco. As a rodeo hero he had the masses behind him, and he again marshalls the people behind him as he takes Rising Star to freedom. The difference, though, is that Sonny is at once both a hero and a villain. The $50,000 reward which Ampco offers for finding Sonny and Rising Star might as well be a "Wanted" poster in the Old West. Sonny lives in an ill-defined world in which he is the hero to some and the villain to others. Given the value system of many Americans, Sonny is not so much a hero as he is a stupid fool to give up all the money he could earn by simply endorsing products. If he is a hero for effectively beating Ampco, then it can only be to himself and to those few who recognize the importance of the principle of his actions. Most will "drive by" and not even recognize him. Sonny is a horse thief, a drunk, a man who strikes women, and a vagabond, yet he is also a man who saves a horse from appearances in Las Vegas. Sort of a hero and sort of a villain, Sonny maintains the wide range of character which typifies all of Pollack's characters.

If anyone should appear to be the object of scorn in *The Electric Horseman*, it should be the executives of Ampco. After all, it is they who reduce former champions to glitter, and they also who make junkies out of champion horses so that they will look good on stage. Yet even big business is not all that bad, although it comes closer to being so here than in any other of Pollack's films. The key here, though, is that the reference is to a corporation rather than to an individual. The individuals themselves do not approach the evil identity of Joubert in *Condor*. Rather, they are men making a living in a most acceptable way. They see that they have mismanaged Rising Star, and they immediately translate that into their mismanagement of Ampco itself. They see that they cannot beat Sonny Steele in spite of all the sophisticated equipment available to them, so they accept the reality of their defeat, although they do attempt to gain some publicity from the event. It is hard to look at the executives of Ampco as villains since they are essentially the individuals who help to put products on shelves. They may use people like Sonny Steele; they may make him a walking display of lights; but Sonny made the actual decision: he signed the contract. Ampco will use him until he becomes a detriment to the corporation, but such is the nature of all big business, which effectively keeps the economy moving. Without an Ampco, Hallie would not have a job because there would be no one to sponsor her television show. The kind of villainy which Ampco displays is perhaps more awful than that which we have seen before because it makes a mockery of an individual, but it is also a very accepted part of the American method of advertising in business. We need only to think of fighters wearing blue bonnets in television commercials.

An Ongoing Illusion

The Electric Horseman provides a suitable temporary conclusion to a review of Sydney Pollack's cinema since this film—like his others—is not so much concluded as it is left open-ended. We do not see the end of an era or the end of a way of life in this film any more than we do in Pollack's other films. We have reached a conclusion, but at the same time we have gone back to the beginning as we look at Sonny as he might have appeared before he entered his first competition.

As the structure of the film lacks an absolute definition, so the nature of good versus bad, weak versus strong, and moral versus immoral similarly lacks absolute definition. They can only be defined by a character in the context of his environment.

While the strength of Sydney Pollack's work as a film director can be seen in the sustained visual excellence, the open-ended structure and the open-ended definitions of character are more crucially important. The image on the screen is, after all, an illusion. But if the illusion is ongoing, and if the characters within it are recognizable in human terms, then the illusion is transmitted into our reality. We walk out of the theater carrying with us not only a vision of America which we recognize, but also a recognition of the potentialities within ourselves whether they are translated into a continued quest for money or a strength to endure against seemingly impossible odds.

Notes and References

Chapter One

1. Aljean Harmetz, "Sydney Pollack: *They Shoot Horses, Don't They?*" *New York Times*, March 8, 1970, section II, p. 13.

Chapter Three

1. Harmetz, II, 13.

Chapter Seven

1. Patricia Erens, "Sydney Pollack," *Film Comment*, September-October 1975, p. 25.

Selected Bibliography

1. Books

GILI, JEAN A., ed. *Sydney Pollack*. Nice: V.E.R. Lettres et Sciences Humaines, 1971. This is the first book written on Pollack, and it contains a series of essays on Pollack's first five films. It also contains an interview with Pollack, and it cites the directors who were probable influences in Pollack's career.

LAPOLLA, FRANCO. *Sydney Pollack*. Firenze: Il Castoro Cinema; La Nuova Italia, 1978. This book is the most recent to be written in Europe. It is a general critical response to Pollack's work in film.

2. Periodicals

"Dialogue on Film: Sydney Pollack." *American Film*, April 1978, pp. 33–48. The interview centers primarily on Pollack's work with actors. He also talks about critics' responses to *Bobby Deerfield* and about his method of achieving the look he wanted for *Jeremiah Johnson*.

ERENS, PATRICIA. "Sydney Pollack." *Film Comment*, September-October 1975, pp. 25–27. This interview elicits responses about some of Pollack's philosophical concerns in the creation of characters. A short interview with Robert Redford is also a part of this article.

———. "Sydney Pollack." *Film Reader*, January 1975, pp. 100–104. Looking at the first five films, the article centers on "Theme and Conflict" and "Circles of Inevitability."

HARMETZ, ALJEAN. "Sydney Pollack: *They Shoot Horses, Don't They?*" *New York Times*, March 8, 1970, section II, p. 13. Coming shortly after the release of *Horses*, this article contains Pollack's responses to reviews of the film as well as the most in-depth biography of Pollack at this time.

SILVERMAN, STEPHEN M. "Comes a Horseman to Las Vegas." *American Film*, May 1979, pp. 16–22. Complete with appropriate pictures of the stars and the locations, this article takes a behind-the-scenes look at the problems of filming in Caesar's Palace and in the unexpected blizzard conditions in Utah. Pollack talks about his work with the actors and his solutions to some of the problems which he had to face.

Filmography

THE SLENDER THREAD (An Athena Production presented by Paramount Pictures, 1965)
Producer: Stephan Alexander
Assistant Director: Don Roberts
Screenplay: Sterling Silliphant
Photography: Loyal Griggs
Production Design: Jack Poplin
Production Manager: Frank Caffey
Editor: Tom Stanford
Costume Design: Edith Head
Music: Quincy Jones
Sound: John Carter
Process Photography: Farciot Eduart
Running Time: 90 minutes
Cast: Sidney Poitier (Alan Newell), Anne Bancroft (Mrs. Inga Dyson), Telly Savalas (Dr. Coburn), Steven Hill (Mark Dyson), Edward Asner (Det. Judd Ridley)
New York Premiere: December 23, 1965, at the Festival, Murray Hill, and Victoria
16mm. rental: Paramount Non-Theatrical Division (Hollywood)

THIS PROPERTY IS CONDEMNED (A Seven Arts, Ray Stark Production in association with Paramount Pictures, 1966)
Producer: John Houseman
Assistant Director: Eddie Saeta
Screenplay: Francis Ford Coppola, Fred Coe, and Edith Sommer
Photography: James Wong Howe
Production Design: Stephen Grimes
Art Direction: Phil Jeffries
Production Manager: Clarence Eurist
Editor: Adrienne Fazan
Costume Design: Edith Head

Music: Kenyon Hopkins
Sound: Harry Lindgren
Process Photography: Farciot Eduart
Running Time: 110 minutes
Cast: Natalie Wood (Alva Starr), Robert Redford (Owen Legate), Charles Bronson (J. J. Nichols), Kate Reid (Hazel Starr), Mary Badham (Willie Starr)
New York Premiere: August 3, 1966, at the Festival and Victoria
16mm. rental: Paramount Pictures Non-Theatrical Division (Hollywood)

THE SCALPHUNTERS (A Levy-Gardner-Laven and Rolan Kibbee Production released through United Artists, 1968)
Producers: Jules Levy, Arthur Gardner, and Arnold Laven
Assistant Director: Keven Donnelly
Screenplay: William Norton
Photography: Duke Callaghan and Richard Moore
Production Design: Frank Arrigo
Production Manager: Henry Spitz and Jack Corrick
Editor: John Woodcock
Costume Design: Joe Drury
Music: Elmer Bernstein
Sound: Jesus Gonzales Gancy
Running Time: 103 minutes
Cast: Burt Lancaster (Joe Bass), Shelley Winters (Kate), Telly Savalas (Jim Howie), Ossie Davis (Joseph Winthrop Lee), Armando Silvestre (Two Crows)
New York Premiere: April 2, 1968, at the Astor, 86th St. East and Neighborhood Showcase Theaters
16mm. rental: United Artists 16 (New York)

CASTLE KEEP (A Filmways Production for Columbia Pictures, 1969)
Producers: Martin Ransohoff and John Calley
Assistant Director: Marc Maurette
Screenplay: Daniel Taradash and David Rayfiel (based on a novel by William Eastlake)
Photography: Henri Decae
Helicopter Photography: Nelson Tyler
Production Design: Rino Mondellini
Art Directors: Max Douy, Jacques Douy, and Morton Rabinowitz
Set Decorations: Charles Merangel
Production Manager: Ludmilla Goulian
Editor: Malcolm Cooke
Costume Design: Jacques Ponteray
Music: Michel Legrand

Sound: Antoine Pettijean
Running Time: 106 minutes
Cast: Burt Lancaster (Major Abraham Falconer), Peter Falk (Sgt. Orlando Rossi), Patrick O'Neal (Capt. Lionel Beckman), Jean Pierre Aumont (Comte de Maldorais), Astrid Heeren (Therese), Scott Wilson (Cpl. Ralph Clearboy), Tony Bill (Lt. Adam B. Amberjack), Michael Conrad (Sgt. Juan De Vaca), Bruce Dern (Lt. Billy Bix), Al Freeman, Jr. (Pfc. Alistair Benjamin)
New York Premiere: July 23, 1969, at Loew's State II and Orpheum
16mm. lease: Columbia 16 (Los Angeles); rental, MacMillan/Audio-Brandon, Budget Films (Los Angeles), and others

THEY SHOOT HORSES, DON'T THEY? (ABC Pictures Corporation presentation of Palomar Pictures and Irwin Winkler, Robert Chartoff, and Sydney Pollack Production, 1969)
Producers: Irwin Winkler, Robert Chartoff, and Sydney Pollack
Assistant Director: Al Jennings
Screenplay: James Poe and Robert Thompson (based on a novel by Horace McCoy)
Photography: Phillip Lathrop
Production Design: Harry Honer
Production Manager: Ed Woehler
Editor: Frederic Steinkamp
Costume Design: Don Feld
Music: John Green
Sound: Tom Overton
Running Time: 121 minutes
Cast: Jane Fonda (Gloria), Michael Sarrazin (Robert), Susannah York (Alice), Gig Young (Rocky), Red Buttons (Sailor), Bonnie Bedelia (Ruby), Bruce Dern (James), Robert Fields (Joel), Allyn Ann McLerie (Shirl)
New York Premiere: March 1970 at the Fine Arts
16mm. rental: Films, Inc. (Wilmette, Illinois)

JEREMIAH JOHNSON (A Wizan-Sanford Production for Warner Brothers, 1972)
Producers: Joe Wizan and Sydney Pollack
Assistant Director: Mike Moder
Screenplay: John Milius and Edward Anhalt (based on the novel *Mountain* by Vardis Fisher, and the story "Crow Killer" by Raymond W. Thorp and Robert Bunker)
Photography: Andrew Callaghan
Production Design: Ted Haworth
Production Manager: John Coonan
Editor: Thomas Stanford

Costume Design: Bernie Pollack
Music: John Rubenstein and Tim McIntire
Sound: Charles Wilburn
Running Time: 108 minutes
Cast: Robert Redford (Jeremiah Johnson), Will Geer (Bear Claw), Steffan Gierasch (Del Gue)
World Premiere: May 9, 1972, at the Cannes Festival
New York Premiere: December 21, 1972, at Loew's Tower East
16mm. rental: MacMillan/Audio-Brandon, Budget Films (Los Angeles), and others

THE WAY WE WERE (Columbia Pictures, 1973)
Producer: Ray Stark
Assistant Director: Howard Koon, Jr.
Screenplay: Arthur Laurents
Photography: Harry Stradling, Jr.
Production Design: Stephen Grimes
Production Manager: Russ Saunders
Editor: Margaret Booth, John Burnett
Costume Design: Dorothy Jeakins and Moss Mabry
Music: Marvin Hamlisch
Title Song: Marvin Hamlisch, Marilyn and Alan Bergman; sung by Barbra Streisand
Sound: Jack Solomon
Running Time: 118 minutes
Cast: Barbra Streisand (Katie Morowsky), Robert Redford (Hubbell Gardiner), Bradford Dillman (J. J.), Lois Chiles (Carol Ann), Patrick O'Neal (George Bisinger), Viveca Lindfors (Paula Reisner), Allyn Ann McLerie (Rhea Edwards), Murray Hamilton (Brooks Carpenter)
New York Premiere: October 17, 1973, at Loew's State 1 and Tower East
16mm. rental: Swank Films (St. Louis)

THE YAKUZA (Warner Brothers, 1975)
Producer: Sydney Pollack
Assistant Director: Mickey Moore
Screenplay: Paul Schrader and Robert Towne
Photography: Okazaki Kozo
Production Design: Stephen Grimes
Art Direction: Ishida Yoshiyuki
Production Manager: John R. Coonan
Editor: Frederic Steinkamp
Costume Design: Dorothy Jeakins
Music: Dave Grusin
Sound: Basil Fenton-Smith

Running Time: 112 minutes
Cast: Robert Mitchum (Harry Kilmer), Brian Keith (George Tanner), Takakura Ken (Tanaka Ken), Herb Edelman (Wheat), Richard Jordan (Dusty), Kishi Keiko (Eiko), Okada Eiji (Tono), James Shigeta (Goro), Kyosuke Mashida (Kato)
New York Premiere: March 19, 1975, at the Beekman and Criterion
16mm. rental: Swank Motion Pictures, St. Louis, Mo.

THREE DAYS OF THE CONDOR (A Dino de Laurentiis Presentation distributed by Paramount Pictures, 1975)
Producer: Stanley Schneider (And Sydney Pollack following the death of Schneider)
Assistant Director: Pete Scoppa
Screenplay: Lorenzo Semple and David Rayfiel
Photography: Owen Roizman
Production Design: Stephen Grimes
Art Director: Gene Rudolf
Production Manager: Paul Granapoler
Editor: Frederic Steinkamp and Don Guidice
Costume Design: Bernie Pollack and Theoni Aldridge
Music: Dave Grusin
Sound: Dennis Maitland
Running Time: 118 minutes
Cast: Robert Redford (Joe Turner), Faye Dunaway (Kathy), Cliff Robertson (Higgins), Max Von Sydow (Joubert), John Houseman (Wabash), Addison Powell (Atwood), Walter McGinn (Barber), Tina Chen (Janice), Michael Kane (Wicks)
New York Premiere: September 24, 1975, at Loew's Astor Plaza and Tower East
16mm. rental: Paramount Pictures Non-Theatrical Division (Hollywood)

BOBBY DEERFIELD (Columbia and Warner Brothers, 1977)
Producer: Sydney Pollack
Assistant Director: Paul Reydor
Screenplay: Alvin Sargent (based on a novel by Erich Maria Remarque)
Photography: Henri Decae
Production Design: Stephen Grimes
Art Direction: Mark Frederix
Production Manager: William Finnegan
Editor: Frederic Steinkamp
Costume Design: Bernie Pollack and Annalisa Nasalli Rocca
Music: Dave Grusin
Sound: Basil Fenton-Smith
Running Time: 126 minutes

Cast: Al Pacino (Bobby Deerfield), Marthe Keller (Lillian), Anny Duperey (Lydia), Walter McGinn (The Brother), Romolo Valli (Uncle Luigi)
New York Premiere: September 29, 1977, at the Baronet and Coronet
16mm. rental: Swank Motion Pictures, St. Louis, Mo.

THE ELECTRIC HORSEMAN (Columbia, Universal, 1979)
Producer: Ray Stark
Assistant Director: Mickey Moore
Screenplay: Paul Gaer and Robert Garland
Photography: Owen Roizman
Production Design: Stephen Grimes
Art Direction: J. Dennis Washington
Production Manager: Ron Schwary
Editor: Sheldon Kahn
Costume Design: Bernie Pollack
Music: Dave Grusin
Sound: Al Overton, Jr.
Running Time: 122 minutes
Cast: Robert Redford (Sonny Steele), Jane Fonda (Hallie), Valerie Perrine (Charlotta), Timothy Scott (Leroy), Nick Coster (Fitzgerald), Willie Nelson (Wendell)
New York Premiere: December 21, 1979, at Loew's Astor Plaza and New York Twin and neighborhood Columbia Premiere Theatres

Index

PN
1998
A3
P5926

Taylor, William
Robert, 1942-

Sydney Pollack